DYNAMICS OF EDUCATIONAL LEADERSHIP
SERIES

STRATEGIC THINKING FOR THE SCHOOL ADMINISTRATOR

HEATHER THANE

Copyright © 2016 Greatness Publishing
All rights reserved.

No portion of this book may be reproduced, stored in a retrieval system or transmitted in any form or by any means – electronic, mechanical, photocopy, recording, or other – except for brief quotations in printed reviews, without prior permission from the publisher.

www.ideasandsolutions.org

Cover Design and Formatting by Farouk J. Roberts

Library and Archives Canada

ISBN: 978-1-927579-15-2

DYNAMICS OF EDUCATIONAL LEADERSHIP
Strategic Thinking for the School Administrator

PRAISE

"Dynamics of Educational Leadership" gives a comprehensive view of many Theories of Leadership and shows how they can be incorporated into Educational Administration at every level of an institution. The exercises given at different stages in the book provides for reflection, internalization, and global application to build an effective and continuously growing institution.

Dr. Elvris Hewitt-Buckle, University Administrator, Jamaica

Leadership is integral to the successful functioning of any organization. In Heather's Book, she outlines not only theoretical principles but practical examples for being a successful leader. Her thoughts are clearly articulated, universal in application, and futuristic.

Cebert Adamson, MSc., Former Executive Director, CCCJ (2009 - 2012); Manager, Programme Quality and Centre for Teaching and Learning, Mohawk College, Ontario, Canada

"Dynamics of Educational Leadership" brings into sharp focus strategies that will reshape the thinking of employees who want to revolutionize the leadership landscape in education and add value to teaching profession globally. If you want to be the catalyst for change, this is a must read!

Dr. Jeneive Marshall-Sommerville, College Administrator, Manchester, Jamaica

An impressive body of work, Heather! School Leaders are expected to hold others accountable. The Teachers' Unions (where they exist) need to support and embrace the Concepts outlined in "Educational Leadership", which are aimed at the abandonment or curtailment of some traditional practices that are no longer productive in the global classroom.

Mr. Wilbert Tomlinson, Managing Director, FACTS Limited, Mandeville, Jamaica

You amaze me! The Contents of this book will make a tremendous difference in the Leadership within Education environments. As a Licenced Educator, I know through experience that the Leadership in a School needs to create positive energy. Education has needs that are universal and all School Leaders globally should read this book and learn about Leadership with a 'positive energy'. You are a Positive Energy Leader. Congratulations!

Charlene Doak-Gebauer, B. Ed., OCT, BBA, Bus. Specialist, Special Education, NNCP, RHN; London, Ontario

Thanks, Heather for a very compact resource document! It covers a wide variety of the SWOT Analysis in the development of the categories of learning through our Educational Institutions from Vice Principals to Department Heads to Students. Also, your book includes an intriguing aspect of the values and development of training which will reflect self-building in a global atmosphere.

While we monitor the Educational programmes and guidelines going forward, it is necessary in the process to take a second look at how we develop our Curriculum for teaching. This useful document is geared to cover broad-based facts on proper Budgeting for self and organizations.

Thanks for your good work!
*Rev. Errol White, B.A. Pastoral Theology, Dip. Pastoral Leadership;
Chaplain for Educational Institution, Jamaica*

The Contents of Heather's book are professionally structured and qualified in its skeletal framework as an excellent tool of systematic academic learning.
Dennis Cassanova, Computer Programmer, Information Technology Practitioner, Mandeville, Jamaica

TABLE OF CONTENTS

Acknowledgments   *ix*
Preface   *x*
Introduction   *xiii*

CHAPTER 1: GLOBAL CONCEPTS OF SCHOOL
LEADERSHIP   1
    40 Leadership Theories/Styles/Approaches
    School Leadership
    Leadership Framework
    Psychometric Testing
    Leadership Reflections

CHAPTER 2: VALUE-ADDED MEASURES FOR
DEPARTMENT HEADS   35
    Academic Planning and Development
    Personnel and Resource Management
    Quality Assurance
    Regulations and Legal Obligations
    Programme Monitoring
    Critical Incidents and Emergency Management
    Using Observations to Improve Quality Instruction
    Feedback to Teachers
    Evaluating Lesson Plans
    Collaborative Programme Delivery
    Team Building – Positive Departmental Culture
    Incorporating the Use of Technology and E-Learning in
    Programme Delivery
    Leadership Reflections

CHAPTER 3: PLANNING MEETINGS AND
COMMUNICATING IN A
TECHNOLOGY-BASED SOCIETY   69

    Forms of Meetings
    Codes of Conduct
    Planning the Meeting
    Roles of Team Members
    Developing the Agenda
    Contents of the Agenda
    Steps in Conducting a Meeting
    Creating School "Base Teams"
    Mock Meeting Activity
    Time Management
    Factors that Derail Meetings
    Observing Protocols
    Physical Setting
    Participation and Attendance
    Robert Rules Order
    Leadership Reflections

CHAPTER 4: STRATEGIC PLANNING IN AN EDUCATIONAL COMMUNITY   91

    Aligning Strategy to Budget
    Financial Planning
    Developing Departmental Budgets
    Budgeting as a Tool to Drive Curriculum Delivery and Student Success
    Budget Review Strategy
    Leadership Reflections

CHAPTER 5: CURRICULUM, INSTRUCTION, AND STUDENT SUCCESS FROM AN INTERNATIONAL PERSPECTIVE   122

    Self-Reflection
    Trust Building Using Paralanguage, Response Behaviour, and Diagnostic Tools
    Mediational Discourse Reflection

Commitment to Student Learning
Performance and Teacher Assessment Progress Reports
Supervision of Instruction
Quality Feedback
Networking and Learning Communities
Peer Review Teacher Assessment
Learning Needs of Students
Resources Used to Improve Teaching and Learning
Differentiation
Formal and Informal Assessments of Instructional Effectiveness of Teachers
Alternative Approaches to Supervision: Coaching and Mentoring
Performance-Based Pay
Building Instructional Capacity
Professional Development
Student-Centred and Learning-Centred Instruction
Using Technology to Support Collaboration
Analyzing Test Results
Leadership Reflections

Summative Exercises for School Administrators	*177*
References	*184*
Contributors' Page	*190*
Other Books by Heather Thane	*192*
About the Arthur	*195*

ACKNOWLEDGMENTS

I appreciate the caring, democratic modelling of Instructional Leaders in Canada, Paul Panayi, Chris Friesen, and Cebert Adamson. Thanks also, for the critical review of the Manuscript they completed during its Drafting. Also, special thanks to George Montague and family, who has been a sounding board for my ideas. I am indebted to Dan Clarke for sharing his thoughtful insights, global perspectives, and classroom experiences. He has also contributed to the External Reviews for my books in a timely manner.

I have been extraordinarily blessed with a supportive and loving family – Gordon, Greg, Cami, and my mother, Dr. Clover Jarrett, who have resolutely and unfalteringly supported my pursuit to complete all seven titles.

The Greatness Publishing Team was Conscientious and Professional in the work carried out.

I am most grateful to Jeneive Marshall-Sommerville, who contributed original works in partnership with me.
Thanks to Paulette McTaggart for her dedication and care in editing this Book.

Lastly, I would like to thank the Church Teachers' College Family for warmly welcoming me into their Institution. I am confirming that the opinions stated in this book are my own, and not the Institute.

PREFACE

The Dynamics of Educational Management Series can be used as a core or supplemental Education Textbook/Workbook for Curriculum and Educational Leadership Courses. It can assist Curriculum Researchers and Thesis or Dissertation Supervisors and Candidates. Finally, it can serve as support for Professional Development for School Improvement Initiatives. The Bodies of Literature consulted for this Guide Series include Instructional Leadership, School Curriculum, Teacher Development, Administrative Leadership, combined with many specialized topics, such as, Technology and Special Education.

My journey to complete this book involved countless hours of Research, and constant dialogue with Global Instructional Leaders. It is strongly recommended that my two other books are utilized as accompanying Textbooks for School Leaders, and employ the Strategies in their Educational Context:
- Teaching Educators to Raise Leaders: 3D Leadership Concept
- Leadership Strategies for Secondary School Teachers

Combined Practices and Experiences of School Administrators are fundamental to the development of expertise in the Learning Environment, as it relates to complex Problem-solving. In preparing individuals for School Leadership positions, formal education needs to include work experiences. School Administration is a complex art which brings together abstract thinking, prior school experience, and action. It is vital that Practitioners engage in Reflection as a process of learning. With the complexity involved in School Life, it is important that School

Leaders examine their own beliefs and values on Teaching and Effective School Leadership. The process of learning how to adjust to various Practical Situations and Experiences and developing Cognitive Skills that can be applied to real-world situations are essential.

Feedback to and from the Instructor is important when combined with the content of this book, in addition to Instructor-based Questions, Reading Assignments, Book Reviews, Self-Assessments, Leadership Reflections that this book provides, Web Activities, Searches, Individual and Group Exercises, and Module Evaluations. This Approach to Leadership Development is created to reflect on Principles, Theories, and Attributes related to Student-centred Practices, and can be found in the "Leadership Reflection" Activities throughout each Chapter.

School Administration involves Leadership Practice. It is the role of the School Leader to be effective, efficient, and encourage staff to demonstrate Core Principles and Best Practices where Students can excel in and beyond School walls. The Roles and Functions of School Leadership, and Reflections included in the Educational and other Leadership Activities are explicitly addressed in some countries. All of the Leadership Practices and Conceptions of the School Leadership Initiatives focus on Improving Education as the core activity of the School. Singapore supports School Leaders in developing competencies including: Leadership, Social, Personal, Educational, and School Development. Leaders are developed through "Thinking Schools" and "Learning Communities." Canadian Providers, in their Guidelines for School Leaders focus on Competence, Task, and Value Orientation, and Training Practicing Leaders to lead efficiently and effectively in a context characterized by Change and Complexity. New Zealand develops Educational Leaders by their Ability to Reflect, Interpersonal Competencies, and Foundation and Values based on their Profession.

It is vital that School Leaders develop an awareness of dealing carefully and responsibly with power and should reflect on the Teachers and the Students being lead. School Improvement Processes in the 21st Century should promote Independent Learning, Cooperation; Commitment; Interpretations of Regulations and Instructions, Decision-Making Process, Conflict Resolution, and Problem-solving. School Leadership Activities need to be brought in line with these fundamental propositions.

This book will guide School Administrators to reflect on Leadership issues, particularly related to Student Achievement, Assessment, Standards, and Accountability, and how these impact on Professional Practice and Decision-making. This Companion Journal offers Leadership Reflection Exercises throughout the Chapters and answers three key questions:

- What else should I know?
- Where do I get support to do this?
- How I can move from knowledge of the concepts to utilizing Strategic Thinking?

This book is packed with forty (40) Leadership Concepts / Styles / Approaches and the Reader will have a feeling of Enthusiasm and Empowerment, as well as being envisioned as Change Agents, supporting the attitudes of Developing Leaders towards Policymaking in the 21st Century.

INTRODUCTION

School Administrators are at the heart of ensuring that Students achieve success in our Schools. When Teachers, Families, and Communities engage in Collaborative Leadership, it provides an opportunity to contribute in significant ways to the Vision of Educational Excellence for all Learners. There is tremendous goodwill and expertise in our Schools and Communities which provides an incredible foundation for powerful Instructional Strategies; School Leaders need to ensure that these Strategies work together in a framework that provides Leadership Structures and Tools to respond appropriately to Student Concerns that face the society now or in the future.

Effective School Leaders hold high expectations, not only for the Students, but for themselves, and for the responsibility in preparing our Students for the global demand of the 21st Century. Data and Research should inform the Education Sector, which will guide Leadership Actions and Plans. Students should have access to Challenging and Relevant Curriculum. The Pedagogy we employ should reflect changes in how we teach Students, which is designed to maximize learning. High-quality Instructional Resources, electronic, digital, and technological resources are required to expand the ability of Parents to communicate with Teachers, actively participate in the Schooling of their children, and participate in decision-making. These Instructional Resources will expand their knowledge of the world.

School Leaders should employ Comprehensive Assessment Systems designed primarily to improve Academic Outcomes for all Students.

Multiple approaches provide a clear purpose of supporting strong Instructions for all Students, including Classroom Observations. Data-driven Planning informs Leaders in Education, Parents, Teachers, Students, and the wider Community how well Students are performing. School Leaders can only accurately and comprehensively determine the required changes when data is available that gives a true picture of Multiple-way Communication, Accountability, and Resources that are aligned with Pedagogical Purposes. It is vital that School Programmes and Services are effectively coordinated and administered which will result in guaranteed Student Results.

School Administrators need to become catalysts and support each other in moving beyond the current Boundaries and Limitations to new Action, in order to inspire successful 21st Century citizens. Effective School Leaders are knowledgeable about what works in their Educational Contexts and seek to develop the capacity to engage in continuous Reflection, which leads to Strategic Thinking. It is fundamental that School Leaders build a sense of Professional Accountability among all practitioners involved in educating Students, including Teachers, Parents, Counsellors, Volunteers, Support Staff, Principals, and other Administrators. Educators can individually and collectively embark on a necessary and important journey of capturing the genius power within each student; this can be accomplished by reflecting and redesigning their approach to Education.

1
GLOBAL CONCEPTS OF SCHOOL LEADERSHIP

Leadership is not a one-size-fits-all approach. It is very essential for Leaders to become familiar with as many Leadership Frameworks as possible, which will add value and flexibility to the Education agenda, both locally and globally. School Administrators must be global-ready to demonstrate Expertise and Leadership to ensure that Students are prepared effectively to be innovators, collaborators, and communicators. It is fundamental that Global attitudes, skills, and knowledge are integrated into the Curriculum, Instruction, and Assessment. Within each individual School, Leadership can contribute to improving Student Outcomes by organizing the ways Teaching and Learning occur. School Leadership designed for the Industrial age has changed with the complex challenges faced in the 21st Century.

Leadership is defined by Leithwood, et al (2006) as establishing directions for an organization which are widely agreed-upon and worthwhile supporting individuals to carry out those directions by doing whatever it takes. Leadership impacts significantly on the quality of the School Organizations and on Student Learning. It is the responsibility of Leaders to "get it right." Educational Leadership Researchers focus exclusively on Leadership in Schools; on the other hand Leadership Researchers concerned with non-school contexts focus their attention on how their Theories and evidence spread across organizational sectors, including Schools.
The dynamics of School Leadership has incorporated more roles to accommodate capacity building in various educational contexts.

Today, School Leaders are required to be both good Instructional Leaders and Administrators and have the ability to focus on Teaching and Learning. It is now more than ever, that School Administrators are being held accountable for how well Teachers and Students learn and, as such, the Education focus has changed over the last decade to accommodate this concept. Because of these changes, School Leaders remain crucially important for continually improving Education.

Mulford (2003) posited that School Leadership is now associated with Public Management and moving away from a Bureaucratic and Institution-led Approach toward Performance-driven, with a new awareness to Service Delivery. Today, the Job Descriptions include Instructional, Moral, Participative, Managerial, and Transformational Leadership. The author posited that School Leaders should have the time and ability to build teams rather than being bothered by Bureaucracy. The ultimate priority of School Leaders is Educational Leadership.

Mid-level and Senior Leadership have the core obligation to have organizational impact. The strong Technical Expertise acquired by Leaders help them to make decisions at this level. The Success of a School Leader is defined and measured to a large extent by the ability to influence, collaborate and promote creativity by working along with other Leaders for high School Achievements.

There is a challenge for Mid-level Managers in Schools to be strategic in their Leadership Roles while undertaking their tactical priorities. Mid-level School Leaders can succeed in their role when they have a School-wide Perspective. It is important to build a network of connections, both inside and outside the School to provide advice, support, and sense of community, which School Leaders can utilize when resilience and resolve gets tested in various ways. These social and educational connections will provide opportunities to impact on global levels.

According to Leithwood, et al (2006), Successful School Leaders can inform Leadership Development Initiatives and serve as one yardstick by which to assess the performance of Leaders. The author argued on the assumptions that all individuals can be good Leaders and Effective Leadership is a learned function. Individuals are capable of being more skilled in most Leadership Functions, but some demonstrate more readiness skills than others and some have much higher capacity levels. The delivery of School Leadership should become more sophisticated and develop individuals who have the potential to achieve at outstanding levels of Leadership.
Leithwood, et al (2006) referred to many External Factors that contribute to shaping the actual Practices of Leaders, including Educational Policies; On-the-Job Leadership Opportunities; Mentoring Experiences; and Professional Development Initiatives. Internal Factors, however, play a significant part in Leadership Practices – their Thoughts, Feelings, Educational Histories, Professional Identity, Values, and Dispositions.

In the past, Definitions of Leadership examined Behaviours of Leaders. The Definitions generally made reference to Leader-Follower Relationships with a focus on Conflict and Power. It was the Behaviours that formed part of the Leadership Training. Thomas Carlyle, Karl Marx, and Gerog Hegel were famous Theorists who contributed their view in the early beginnings, which included, Leaders were Born, not Made and that Leaders emerged from Social and Economic Settings of their time. The Historic

Definitions showed that Leaders have loyal and committed Followers and should not be seen independent of each other (Weller, et al. 2001).

LEADERSHIP REFLECTION

Reflect on your Leadership for TWO - FOUR hours.
Describe your Leadership Performance during the past two months?

_____
_____
_____
_____
_____
_____
_____
_____
_____
_____
_____
_____
_____

Outline TWO (2) Critical Decisions you have made in the past two years

_____
_____
_____
_____

State the Added-Value you brought to those you Supervised?

Identify a minimum of FIVE of your Strengths and Weaknesses

_____
_____
_____
_____
_____
_____
_____
_____
_____
_____
_____
_____
_____
_____
_____
_____
_____
_____
_____
_____
_____

Discuss THREE Ways that you Strengthened the Sense of Community among School Leaders?

_____
_____
_____
_____
_____

According to Weller, et al (2001), Leaders are responsible for Planning, Delegating, Coordinating, and Motivating. School Leaders need to acquire the knowledge and skills of a Leader. Leaders utilize power to influence the Behaviour of individuals, as pioneered by French and Raven (1968). The Author argued that Reward Power is provided by Leaders in the form of Promotions and Praise; Expert Power is special abilities acquired by Leaders that are sought after by their Followers, such as, Education; Referent Power is the ability to lead through Charisma relating to respect and presence of the Leader; Legitimate Power is sanctioned by the Organization which is dictated by the position held in the

Organization; and Coercive Power is the use of Punishment as a method to get individuals to perform.

All five Sources of Power can be used by School Leaders in several contexts, outlined in the Table below. The Knowledge of these Sources of Power can assist School Leaders as they carry out their tasks in the relevant settings.

GOALS OF SCHOOL	TASKS	SOURCES OF POWER
ASSIGNMENT OF SUBJECTS/COURSES TO TEACHERS BASED ON ABILITY LEVELS	Conducting Performance-Based Evaluations	Coercive Power Reward Power
PERMISSION AND FUNDS TO ATTEND CONFERENCES/WORKSHOPS AND ACQUIRING MATERIALS	Granting Leave of Absence	Legitimate Power Coercive Power
EVALUATION PROCESS	Making Objective, Unbiased Teacher Evaluations	Legitimate Power Expert Power Reward Power Coercive Power
HIRING	Selecting Best Candidate	Expert Power
PROMOTION RECOMMENDATIONS	Appointing Candidates for Administrative Positions	Referent Power Coercive Power Legitimate Power
TENURE RECOMMENDATIONS	Managing Tenure Issues	Expert Power Legitimate Power Referent Power

LEADERSHIP THEORIES

YUKL'S TAXONOMY

According to Leithwood, et al (2006), important Leader and Manager Behaviours were classified by Yukl (1994). The fourteen Behaviours include Planning and Organizing, Problem-solving, Clarifying Roles and Objectives, Informing, Monitoring, Motivating and Inspiring, Controlling, Delegating, Supporting, Developing and Mentoring, Managing Conflict ad Team Building, Networking, Recognizing, and Rewarding. Leithwood, et al (2006) stated that these Managerial Behaviours compared with the four Core Practices of Successful School Leadership – Setting Directions, Developing People, Redesigning the Organization, and Managing the Teaching Programme.

Leithwood, et al (2006) provided the following brief synopsis of the Alternative Leadership Theories:

Ohio State Model highlights two Styles: Task-oriented and Supportive. The Effectiveness of each Style depends on Variables, such as, size of organization and clarity of roles.

Contingency Theory is similar to the Ohio State Model whereby it seeks to explain Leadership Effectiveness in terms of Task or Relationship Style. To be most effective, the setting in which the Leaders find themselves need to be matched with the Leadership Styles.

Participative Leadership Model focuses on how Leaders engage individuals in Organizational Decisions. Leaders select among three distinct Approaches: Autocratic Approach allows for Low Member Participation; Consultative Approach occurs when Participation is restricted to providing information; and Collaborative Sharing promotes extensive Participation. Decision Quality, Minimized Costs, and Time will determine which Approach is utilized.

Situational Leadership occurs where the Leader engages in a more Relationship Approach and effective when the Followers move towards high levels of Maturity.

Path-Goal Theory describes Leadership as being Supportive, Directive, Participative, or Achievement-Oriented, depending on the Situation. This Theory promotes opportunities for satisfaction. Vertical Dyad Linkage Model, Leader-Member Exchange (LMX) Theory, and Individualized Leadership Theory are presented in the form of a Multi-dimensional Approach. The Vertical Dyad Linkage Model recognizes that members of the same group are treated differently. With the development of the Leader-Member Exchange, all members of the group have the same relationship with Leaders. A unique one-to-one relationship developed with the Leaders and their individual colleagues as they influence each other. The focus was placed on the individual rather than the group which led to the Individualized Leader Theory development. The Leader promoted self-worth by investing in Followers and the Followers, in turn, invested in the Leader.

Transformational and Charismatic Leadership are closely related Leadership Types that communicate a captivating vision, high performance expectations, self-confidence, collective purpose, and identity. Socialized Charismatic Leaders are Transformational and their high levels of trust, loyalty, respect, and commitment translate into a tremendous improvement in an organization. Personalized Charismatic Leaders, on the other hand, can be perceived as serving their own interests.

Substitutes for Leadership Approach characterizes organizations engaging in either Task-oriented or Relationship-oriented Functions. Each Organizational Setting requires the Leader to either enhance or neutralize the influence of people. The Leader will attempt to promote Task-Oriented Leadership when tasks are highly standardized and routine, work groups are cohesive and special distance lies between Leaders and Followers. Whereas for Relationship-oriented Leadership, the Leader seeks to utilize in settings where there is a need for independence and professional orientation by colleagues.

Romance of Leadership is related to the Leadership View of the Follower. There is a persuasion of one another of the importance of Leadership. A social transmission of thoughts, ideas, and behaviours to a group of individuals plays an important role in this process.

Self-Leadership has the desired effect of building Leadership Capacities. Employee Empowerment is the highlight of Self Leadership. Individuals and groups involved in this Conception of Leadership Type have the potential to reduce the Resources devoted to traditional practices of Leadership and Supervision.

Multiple Linkage Theory was introduced by Yukl (1994). This Theory recognized the complexity of Formal Organizations and sought to incorporate other Theories to gain a better understanding of how organizations work. In the short-term, the Leader relied on utilizing intervening variables to skillfully correct deficiencies. Situational Variables were utilized by the Leader as a more favoured approach when addressing group performance in the long-term.

TRAIT THEORY

Leaders have many characteristics, and according to White (n.d.), Theorists view individuals as Natural Leaders. It was further stated that it is through the study of Trait Theory that organizations find the correct Leader for the position or organization. Future Leaders may be trained once Leadership Traits are identifiable traits, which led to Research experiencing problems after several years of study.

BEHAVIOURAL THEORY

In the Summary of the Behavioural Theory, the main focus is on the action of the Leader rather than on qualities. Leaders may be Task-oriented or Relationship-oriented depending on the Situation. Some Followers need to be directed, while others require nurture and support (White, n.d.).

SERVANT THEORY

The Concept of Servant Leadership was introduced in the 1960's and 1970's by Robert Greenleaf. Christian Leaders provided some hope to volatile issues, while demonstrations and violence were taking place. The Robert Greenleaf adapted the idea of Servant Leadership whereby serving became an important factor for the Leader (White, n.d.), and simply meeting the needs of the Team by leading with high integrity and generosity.

TRANSACTIONAL LEADERSHIP

According to White (n.d.), Transactional Leadership involves a multi-dimensional model that focuses on Contingent Reward, Management by Exception (Active), and Management by Exception (Passive). Employees are rewarded when they accomplish the goals of the organization, therefore they are judged on performance. Employees are actively monitored for errors and the Leader tries to make corrections or takes a passive role by waiting for employees to make errors and then tries to correct those errors.

PASTORAL LEADERSHIP

White (n.d.) stated that the Concept of Pastoral Leadership is characterized by Casting a Vision, Mobilizing, and Empowering Followers to work together to achieve their goal; transforming lives; experiencing a sense of calling from God; and discovering and utilizing their Spiritual Gifts for their communities. Pastoral Leadership has a direct connection to Transformational Leadership. For its effectiveness, there needs to be trust and inspiration.

INSTRUCTIONAL LEADERSHIP

Leithwood, et al (2006) stated that Successful Leadership involves expertise in Pedagogical content Knowledge Reforms to be implemented in schools and a rich understanding of how to support Teachers in acquiring such knowledge themselves. Leaders require knowledge of how the subject is learned and taught. It is vital that Reform-minded Leaders support both Teachers and

Learners to acquire the new complex Content Knowledge.

EXEMPLARY LEADERSHIP

Exemplary Leadership is referred to as Creative Problem-solving. When exercising Leadership in Schools, expertise in both effective and efficient problem-solving is required. School Leaders are expected to solve problems quickly with few errors by spending time to interpret problems. The Leaders will have access to knowledge of well-structured problems in long-term memory and how to solve them, unlike ill-structured problems. Therefore, the Leader needs to respond in a more deliberate, thoughtful manner when involved in solving ill-structured problems than when solving well-structured problems. School Leaders tend to remain calm and treat staff with genuine respect during interactions, when they acquire skills to solve ill-structured problems (Leithwood et al, 2006).

West Virginia Department of Education (n.d.) in the Summary of Strategic Leadership, discussed the following Theories – Strategic, Cultural, Managerial, Human Resource, and School/Community/Family Leadership:

STRATEGIC LEADERSHIP

Strategic Leadership views School Leadership as preparing Students in the 21st Century for the unseen. A climate of inquiry is created to implore the School Community to build on its core values and beliefs and to chart a path to reach their Goals. The Activities utilized to communicate the core belief, vision, and mission of the School includes Symbols, Stories, and Ceremonies. The School

Leader that establishes goals that reflect demographic data of the Students, Families, and Student Achievement is practicing Strategic Leadership Concept.

CULTURAL LEADERSHIP

Culture plays an important role in Student Achievement and School Improvement. Fundamental to the Cultural Leadership Concept is Fairness, Dignity, and Respect. High expectations for Self, Students, and Staff are features of this Cultural Concept.

MANAGERIAL LEADERSHIP

In support of the Goals of the Strategic Plan, the School Leader utilizing the Managerial Leadership monitors the Budget, Human Resource Allocation, and Material Resources. The Leader in Education should ensure that operational procedures are in place which reinforces clear expectations, structures, and rules for Students and Staff. The Managerial Leader incorporates Technology in managing School Operations and protects information by maintaining confidentiality and privacy of School Records.

HUMAN RESOURCE LEADERSHIP

Human Resource Leaders create processes and systems that promote various activities, including Recruitment, Evaluation, Support, and Development and Retention of High Performing Staff. This Approach is characterized by individuals who are highly visible in the School. The Mission of the Human Resource Leader also includes Induction and Mentoring Skills for New Teachers and

Aligning Professional Development Activities with 21st Century Curriculum, Instruction, and Assessment Needs.

SCHOOL/COMMUNITY/FAMILY LEADERSHIP

The Central Focus for the School Leader, based on the School/Community/Family Leadership is Participation of Stakeholders which creates opportunities for Parents, Community, and Business Representatives. Parents are invited to be active participants in School-level decision-making as part of School Improvement Initiatives. School Leaders, who practice this Leadership Approach, understand the legal process and utilizes it to protect Student Rights and improve Student Opportunities.

MORAL LEADERSHIP

According to "Growing Tomorrow's Leaders Today", Effective Leaders demonstrate Ethical and Moral Leadership. Ethical Moral Leaders promote integrity and courage in difficult situations and seek to make a difference in the lives of Students, remaining focused and purposeful. From this perspective, Moral Leaders are consistent in their beliefs.

APPRECIATIVE LEADERSHIP

One of the most powerful tools for Appreciative Leadership (Whitney, et al, n.d.) is positive questions that promote Empowerment, Risk Taking, and Guiding Value-Based Performance. The Practice of Appreciative Leadership focuses on strengths and positive possibilities, building bridges across departments, organizations, and communities, and releasing cultures of inquiry. The Five Strategies of Appreciative Leadership is based on high performance which includes individuals having a feeling of belonging, feeling valued for what they can contribute, having a sense of where the organization or community is headed, knowing that excellence is expected and can be depended on, and knowing that their contribution is to the greater good.

Changing Minds (2015) outlined the following six Emotional Leadership Styles – Pacesetting, Coaching, Commanding, Affiliative, Visionary, and Democratic:

PACESETTING LEADERSHIP

The key attributes for this Approach is "Lead by Example." Followers are not asked to perform tasks that the Leader would not do, but if they perform poorly they are expected to improve or they are replaced. Positive feedback is limited because of time constraint. Leaders adopting this Approach achieve results in the short-term, however, some Followers get overwhelmed with speed.

COACHING LEADERSHIP

Leaders who entertain conversations that extend beyond the workplace, and delegate challenging assignments are referred to as Coaching Leaders. Focusing on the Strengths and Weaknesses of their Followers, allow Leaders to match each individual to career aspirations and actions. This Approach is best used when Leaders need to build long-term capabilities in the organization.

COMMANDING LEADERSHIP

Commanding Leadership Concept is characterized by Leaders giving clear direction expecting maximum compliance. It is often used when there is a need for fast action and in challenging situations. However, there tends to be a cold and distant feeling experienced from this type of Leader.

AFFILIATIVE LEADERSHIP

An Affiliative Leader embraces a Collaborative Approach to Leadership and focuses on the Emotional Needs of the Follower. The Leader avoids negative Feedback which is distressing to the Follower, therefore creating harmony within the organization. Overall, this Approach reaps positive results.

VISIONARY LEADERSHIP

Leaders share their Vision of the Goals with Followers, but not how to achieve the Goals. There is a sense of Motivation by the Follower when a new direction is required, when the Leader embarks on this Approach. Knowledge Power is passed on to others within the organization.

DEMOCRATIC LEADERSHIP

Participation is the central focus for the Leader adopting the Democratic Leadership Approach. The Leader values the inputs and contributions from their Followers. It is beneficial when the Leader seeks to gain a buy-in on a particular idea. Effectiveness is achieved when ideas or suggestions are put into action.

LAISSEZ-FAIRE LEADERSHIP

A Laissez-faire Leader is described by Martin (2009) as someone who accepts no responsibility in guiding or engaging Followers. There is little intervention by the Leader. The Leaders who employ the Laissez-faire Leadership Approach avoid decision-making and problem-solving, often absent, and fail to follow-up with requests for assistance. Laissez-faire Leadership resembles Passive Management-by-Exception.

DISTRIBUTED LEADERSHIP

Hackmann (n.d.) argued that Distributed Leadership utilizes multiple guidance and direction, which does not mean that no one is responsible for the overall performance of the organization. The primary responsibilities of the Administrative Leader include enhancing the skills and knowledge of individuals establishing a common culture of expectations; combining the various pieces of the organization in a productive relationship; and holding individuals accountable for their contributions. Opportunities are created for individuals to lead in various roles, thereby Sustaining Leadership Capacity. The Leader can make an impact on School Performance in different ways when adopting the Distributed Leadership Approach. The organization experiences a shift from the Traditional "Hierarchical" Model to a Collaborative-type Leadership Approach.

DISTRIBUTED LEADERSHIP CHECKLIST

	YES	NO	COMMENT
Are Teachers accustomed to being Followers?			
Does the Community expect that the Principal is primarily responsible for Leadership?			
Do Administrators prefer to hold on to the Leadership Roles in an effort not to lose power?			
Are Teachers with Leadership Skills willing to reduce Teaching Time to Train others?			
Are Teachers willing to be released from their Teaching Responsibilities for developing their Leadership Skills?			

LEADERSHIP REFLECTION

Visualize your School Culture embracing Distributive Leadership. Identify THREE Barriers that exist within your School Context, which limits your effectiveness implementing the Distributive Leadership Approach

_____
_____
_____
_____
_____
_____

Discuss TWO Ways to overcome the challenges discussed in Part (a)

SCHOOL LEADERSHIP

Pont, et al (2008) posited that School Leadership can include individuals occupying various roles and functions, such as, Principals, Leadership Teams, School Governing, and School Level Staff involved in Leadership Tasks. The School Leader plays a key role in improving Classroom Practice, School Policies, and connections between individual schools and the outside world. The key tasks for School Leadership to improve Teaching and Learning within Schools include, supporting and developing Teacher Quality, defining goals and measuring progress, strategic resource management, and collaboration with external partners. It is important that School Leaders are aware of their role of connecting and adapting Schools to their surrounding environments.

Historically, School Leaders evolved from Practising Teachers with added Responsibilities to Head Teachers and Bureaucratic Administrators, to Professional Managers, and today, Leaders of Learning. The added responsibilities, according to Pont, et al (2008), included Supervising Buildings. Increased Industrialization resulted in the need for more Systematic School Organizations and there was need then for part-time or full-time Administrators at the School Level. In the 20th Century, Principals were hired in the role of Branch Manager which reflected Industrial Development. Throughout most of the 20th Century, the Principal was viewed as the Bureaucratic Administrator or Head Teacher or a combination of the two, with overall responsibilities for the overall operation of the School and Project Implementation. The Principal now became accountable for use of resources in compliance with Government Legislations, Regulations, and Guidelines. As Head Teacher, the Teaching Responsibilities were scaled down to Non-Teaching

Tasks, such as, managing resources, and communicating with Parents and other elements in the Education System. It was clear that Teachers were the Instructional Experts and left on their own. Let us examine the new thrust for School Leaders as it relates to Decentralization, Autonomy, Accountability, and a renewed focus on Teaching and Learning. Decentralization provides the opportunity for School Leaders to engage in more communication, cooperation, and coalition building. Principals are required to develop strong networking and collaboration connections and engage with their peers. Teaching Staff, Parents, and Community Members are frequently involved in School Level Decision-Making. There will be more time available to devote to Human and Financial Resource Management and Instructional Leadership.

Principals, in delegating responsibilities to the School Level, increase their Autonomy to fulfill responsibilities that required expertise which they quite often did not have through formal training, such as, Establishing Budgeting and Accounting Systems; Selecting and Ordering Materials; Developing Relationships with Contractors and Vendors; and Designing Recruitment Schemes. The Role of the Principal became more time-consuming and Pont, et al (2008) argued that the position included Administrative and Managerial workload.

The Financial and Personnel Responsibilities have allowed School Leaders less time to focus on Teaching and Learning, whereby creating new obligations for them to perform at defined standards and expectations. School Leaders are Accountable for performance outcomes of Teachers and Students. There is added Paperwork which resulted in time constraints for School Leaders because of the demands for careful recording, documenting, and communicating developments at both School and Student Levels. The School Leaders are expected to be more strategic and data driven and are involved in planning processes that align curricula to central mandated standards. Clearly, School Administrators need to be open and accountable for what is done within the School.

LEADERSHIP REFLECTION

Identify TWO Leadership Activities in which your Staff is involved in your School

_____
_____
_____
_____

In the Table below, select TWO of your Staff Members performing Leadership Activities and indicate their Knowledge, Skills, and Capacity to Lead

LEADERSHIP ACTIVITIES	KNOWLEDGE	SKILLS	CAPACITY TO LEAD

LEADERSHIP FRAMEWORK

According to The Leadership Framework for Principals and Vice Principals (2014), School Leaders can follow the Guidelines in order to experience success:
- Setting Directions
- Building Relationships and Developing People

- Developing the Organization to Support Desired Practices
- Improving the Instructional Programme
- Securing Accountability

SETTING DIRECTIONS

It is crucial that School Leaders create high expectations for Teachers, Students, and themselves. Success at the School Level can be achieved with frequent reference to the Goals of the School, when engaged in decision-making. Effective Leaders articulate their overall Vision and Goals to Stakeholders.

In support of The Ontario Leadership Framework, the authors of Growing Tomorrow's Learners Today (n.d.) argued that Educational Leaders should convince Students that they can achieve their goals by promoting high expectations. School Leaders need to inspire the trust of Teachers in improving the academic achievement in their Students. Teachers should be encouraged to set academic expectations and work hard to get their Students to internalize those expectations. Utilizing a variety of Learning Styles can arouse Students and support those with lagging academic skills in the classroom. Leaders of Education know how to build upon and sustain Vision.

LEADERSHIP REFLECTION

State TWO Ways that you ensure that ALL Students achieve success

_____
_____

CASE STUDY

Jada had difficulty focusing in class. Anytime the Teacher tried to give her personal attention, she always stated that efforts to get her to understand were a waste of time. The Teacher expressed how he felt whenever she heard him speak in that way. The Teacher asked her one day, for the reason for her utterances. Her response seemed alarming to the Teacher when she expressed that other Teachers are frustrated when she takes a longer time to process the material. Jada was accustomed to sitting quietly and observing other Students reap the benefits of Individualized Attention.

As an Instructional Leader, discuss TWO Strategies that the Teacher utilizes to support Jada.

BUILDING RELATIONSHIPS AND DEVELOPING PEOPLE

Leaders in Education build-upon and respond to the unique needs and expertise of Staff Members and recognize their accomplishments. It is the responsibility of the School Administrators to listen to the ideas of Staff, encourage them to continually re-examine the extent to which their Practices support the learning of all Students, and imploring them to engage in new Practices consistent with School Goals. Visibility of School Values and Practices is of prime importance.

The Concept of Building Relationships is an important element discussed in the New York State Article, Growing Tomorrow's Leaders Today (n.d.). It was stated that School Leaders recognize individual talents and assign responsibility and authority for specific tasks. Leaders in Education should support, develop, and nurture staff.

DEVELOPING THE ORGANIZATION TO SUPPORT DESIRED PRACTICES

It is fundamental that Leaders in Education involve staff in the design and implementation of important school decisions and establish Teams that collaborate on problem-solving (The Ontario Leadership Framework, 2013). It was further stated in the Guidelines that School Leaders should embrace productive relationships with families and connect with the wider community including outreach groups, policy experts, and organizational research agencies. In support of Desired Practices, School Administrators should provide Teachers with Leadership Opportunities, implement and monitor the use of appropriate Disciplinary Practices in the Classroom, ensure effective oversight and Accountability of Resources to support priorities, and maintain a safe and healthy environment.

According to New York State Article, Growing Tomorrow's Leaders Today (n.d.), School Leaders seek to improve the organization through thorough planning. It is important for Leaders in Education to demonstrate respect for Accountability and Responsibility. Effective School Leaders possess skills that manage resources effectively and efficiently.

IMPROVING THE INSTRUCTIONAL PROGRAMME

Fundamental to School Leadership are Providing Support and Time for Collaboration, Building Trusting Relationships, and Creating a Shared Vision. As Instructional Leaders, it is vital to coordinate what is taught by engaging in Classroom Observations and when making School Improvement Decisions, data should be incorporated effectively. School Leaders should monitor all out-of-classroom activities to the Learning Priorities of the School (The Ontario Leadership Framework, 2013). Supporting sustained Professional Development and understanding good Pedagogy and effective Classroom Practices are also valuable skills for the School Leader (Growing Tomorrow's Leaders Today, n.d.).

SECURING ACCOUNTABILITY

According to The Ontario Leadership Framework (2013), assisting staff in making connection between School Goals and Ministry Goals is an effort for School Leaders to strengthen commitment. Schools are expected to meet the demands for External Accountability and School Performance should be transparent to all Stakeholders, such as, Ministry, Board, Parents, and Community. The New York State Article, Growing Tomorrow's Leaders Today (n.d.), was in support in stating that School Leaders work to win support even when there is awareness that not all individuals will support change. Leaders will have to develop the courage to take informed risks.

PSYCHOMETRIC TESTING

Assessing and appraising individuals in Schools are processes that are highly complex and subjective. Psychometric Tests are a great way of objectively assessing the "hidden" traits of an individual. The Tests provide a great deal of reliable information to make important personnel decisions.

School Leaders can utilize Psychometric Tests to determine how best to improve current performance and skills of their Teachers. Many of these tests are completed online and assist in uncovering value and interests that are fundamental to overall job satisfaction. Individuals can take the Test anytime, and anywhere, and get accurate results anytime.

Psychometric Tests can measure Interest, Personality, and Aptitude, as summarized in the following Table:

TESTS	MEASUREMENTS
Interest	How Individuals differ in motivation, values, and opinions
Personality	How Individuals differ in their actions
Aptitude	How Individuals differ in their ability to carry out various tasks

Personnel and Career-related Assessments are more objective when Psychometric Tests are prescribed and some of the benefits of these Tests are enumerated below:
- Saves time
- Easy to administer to individuals or groups of individuals
- Easy to score
- Quick and reliable results

LEADERSHIP REFLECTION

Reflect on the most challenging Instructional Change Process in your School or Region. With the use of examples, describe the Process Changes that were involved and steps that were taken to resolve these issues.

_____
_____
_____
_____
_____
_____
_____

Outline the Strategies being used at your School to support Aspiring and Practicing School Leaders in their changing roles:

Social

Cultural

Economic

Political

___

Create a List of FIVE Multiple Roles of the Dynamic School Leader

___

Speculate on your School in 2030 and your Role as Instructional Leader. Consider yourself as the following:

Resource Personnel

___

Counsellor

_____
_____
_____
_____

Motivator

_____
_____
_____
_____

Mentor

_____
_____
_____
_____

Subject Matter Specialist

_____
_____
_____
_____

Information-giver

2
VALUE-ADDED MEASURES FOR DEPARTMENT HEADS

Department Heads spend a large part of their day to respond to questions and assist in problem solving. It is important that the Teachers in the Department are engaged in discussions on curricula and pedagogical issues, and focusing on student achievement and the role of the Department as it relates to the goals of the whole school. Departments viewed as professional communities that shape the abilities of Teachers in teaching and learning.

Value-added Measures track the "value" that Department Heads add to Individual Student Growth from grade to grade, which have long-term benefits for all Educators and Policymakers. Value-added information is a powerful School Improvement Tool and recognizes the effects of Good Teaching. Evaluating the quality of teaching is one of the roles of the Department Head, in which they provide substantive Curriculum Leadership, focusing on Supervision and Evaluation of Teachers in their Departments. School Administration needs to work closely with Department Heads to understand the scope of the work of each Teacher within the Department and the whole school. The Department Heads should feel empowered and entitled to lead the members in their Department; Both Managerial and Leadership Roles assist in supporting their colleagues.
It is difficult to conceptualize quality teaching and learning without Department Heads. Teachers would benefit greatly from this guidance and expertise. Principals would be outdated in many subject areas and be overwhelmed, and Programmes discontinued,

in the absence of Department Heads. Effective planning and evaluating will ensure a consistently high-quality approach, and hence the need for Department Heads.

By definition, Leadership is the means, will, or power to influence people, and Paranosic (2014) agreed that Department Heads have the potential to lead within a School and are active Leaders in the School; serve as a measure of power and authority for timetable purposes essentially; advice and council sought by others as a form of direction for School; and shape and provide the Department with a vision.

Today, School Leadership reflects on the new roles for mid-level managers which entail monitoring teaching and standards in Departments. The new thrust is for mid-level managers to have the required skills to lead utilizing a range of strategies to build effectiveness which influences structure, cultures, pedagogy, expectations, staffing, and capacity building (Hill, et al. 2008). It is crucial that effective Leaders possess the following characteristics:

- Innovative – Leads by new ideas
- Enthusiastic – Leads with passion, commitment, hard work, energy, motivation
- Approachable – Leads by awareness of the needs of Students
- Determined and Decisive – Leads with high expectations
- Communicator – Leads effectively in managing day-to-day activities and responsible for decision making
- Quality-oriented – Leads with excellence

The Department Head is responsible for supporting Students, Teachers, and Administration which is necessary to facilitate school organization and student success; it involves a complex set of interpersonal communication skills, strongly developed knowledge of curriculum and instruction, and honed collaborative abilities. The ability to deal with stress and support the needs of others, are prerequisites to their outlined roles. Becoming a Department Head is a process and starts with the simple notion of leading and managing (Clarke, 2009).

ACADEMIC PLANNING AND DEVELOPMENT

The Academic Leader contributes to the achievement of the strategic plans of the Department. Clarke (2009) stated that Heads of Department considered themselves to be primarily teachers with a focus on student success. In a study, Department Heads identified one of their most defining role as a Teacher, with a full teaching load, completing supervisory duties in hall and other locations, covering for colleagues in their absence, implementing curriculum, and developing sound instructional practice and management strategies for their classrooms.

PERSONNEL AND RESOURCE MANAGEMENT

Department Heads manage and engage in Administrative Duties, which can be time-consuming. Research suggests that effective Administrators set the climate in the school, through their own willingness to collaborate, make transparent decisions, and engage Department Heads meaningfully in whole school decision- making. It is important that Department Heads surround themselves with an informal network of supports; individuals who can provide insights and suggestions. Fostering Capacity Building is essential for strengthening individuals to perform at their best and ensuring that weaknesses are compensated by the strengths of others.

QUALITY ASSURANCE

Department Heads provide teaching materials and act as a personal resource by providing professional development to colleagues, locate and disseminate information, discuss teaching materials, and share innovative research and new information in various subject areas. Effective Department Heads demonstrate their own immediate value to Department Members. The Department Head adds value by participating in curriculum meetings, continued awareness of available resources, and keeping abreast with the pedagogical happenings in various subject areas. Also, the roles of arranging workshops and meetings, and sharing with other Departments and Regional Offices will ensure high standards of teaching and learning. This quantum leap for middle managers to move to be proactive rather than reactive is a clear indication of setting targets for Professional Development and Improvement.

It is crucial that Department Heads play a major role to School Improvement by contributing to policy development. The new responsibilities for Middle Managers that have emerged in recent years, focuses on managing people rather than resources. There was an assumption that young teachers had knowledge of how work should be done and what work they should be doing. The Department Heads, while preparing for their own teaching, administrative duties, paperwork, and discipline, is called upon to devote substantial time and energy in influencing the quality teaching of others.

REGULATIONS AND LEGAL OBLIGATIONS

The Education Regulations of 1980 governs the Education System.

Academic Leader must be knowledgeable about the laws governing various areas of School Operations. The Education Regulations outline:

- Personnel Laws
- Laws concerning School Operations

Hurley (2001) stated the duties of Vice Principals, Department Heads, Grade Coordinators, and Senior Teachers in Jamaica.

SCHOOL LEADERS	DUTIES
Vice Principals	Supervision of Students, Teachers, and other Personnel Requisition and distribution of school supplies and equipments School record-keeping and statistics Guidance of new Teachers Student discipline and guidance Supervision of extra-curricular activities Specific teaching assignments
Department Heads	Coordination of the work of Departments Assignment of Teacher workloads Leadership of Curriculum Development efforts Assessment of methods of instruction and student evaluation practices Review of Lesson Plans
Grade Supervisors	Coordination of work of class

	teachers and form teachers Work to assure the smooth operation of the School Programme
Senior Teachers	Coordination of extra-curricular activities Organization of Social Programmes Assistance of Staff Welfare, Plant Maintenance, and Guidance of new Teachers

REFLECTIVE PRACTICE

What are the FIVE most important Skills that you must possess to improve the Quality and Diversity of Instruction in your School?

_____
_____
_____
_____
_____
_____
_____
_____
_____
_____

Discuss THREE Strategies that you can utilize to help Teachers view Evaluation as a way of improving Instructional Opportunities for Students?

PROGRAMME MONITORING

Clarke (2009) stated that mentorship is an element that defines the role of Department Heads in terms of supporting individual Teachers, providing guidance and encouragement, engaging in meaningful collaboration, and acting as a source of information and teaching materials. Department Heads are also engaged in several managerial elements. It was further stated that a Department Head acts as a liaison with Administration, which involves taking information between Departments and Administration, providing feedback and suggestions, and collaborating with both sides to garner understanding and expectations. Administrative duties can be a time-consuming role of the Department Head. These duties involve ordering and storing items; organizing staff rooms, classrooms, office space; and accounting for department resources, budgets, and timetables. The skills necessary to manage in this administrative capacity are strong organization and interpersonal skills.

The Administration will benefit from Strategies and Programmes that Academic Leaders implement to meet objectives that will increase student success. Working collaboratively with Administration will ensure that Teachers get information that is needed specific to the Department. When information is shared, challenges existing in schools, such as, failures in standardized tests, can be analyzed at both the Departmental and the Administration levels.

CRITICAL INCIDENTS AND EMERGENCY MANAGEMENT

School Personnel have moral and legal responsibilities to all Students in their care. Schools serve as a "shelter" for hundreds of individuals who live or work nearby, after a disaster is experienced. It is vital that the Academic Leader recognizes safety as the policy of the School. Critical Incidents describe events which threaten to endanger the safety or health of any person, school, or property. It is the responsibility of the Principal to oversee management of all foreseeable Incidents; the Critical Incidents and Emergency Management Plan includes a chain of command outlining responsibilities of Team Members. Checklists are usually designed to ensure all situations are attended to. Academic Leaders should insist that the School Community familiarizes itself with the Critical Incidents and Emergency Management document. This will result in better prepared School Communities, should an emergency occur in the School.

The Principal is usually the CIE Coordinator of the Management Team and is responsible for:
- Policy Review
- Provision of Practice and Professional Development

- Opportunities for School Community Members
- Establishment of preventative measures and coordination of Response Procedures

The Management Team should ensure that:
- Staff Members are well informed
- Prevention and mitigation of emergencies are of prime importance
- Individuals who are traumatized, have recovered
- Updates are received by all relevant members of staff at the start of each year and sent to Departments

The Procedural Checklist below is a framework designed to assist in Managing Incidents and ensure safety and security measures are followed:

_____	Ensure Safety and Security Measures
_____	Identify and confirm those involved
_____	Contact local and external agencies to coordinate efforts
_____	Communication Strategy

Key Personnel:

_____	Student Body
_____	School-wide
_____	Families
_____	Local Community
_____	Broader Community
_____	Coordinate Support (Counselling, Medical)
_____	Post-Crisis Response (Student)
_____	Post-Crisis Response (School)
_____	Post-Crisis Response (Family)
_____	Assessment and Evaluation

It is critical to establish networks when dealing with emergencies. Administrators need to have accurate information so that the proper information is passed on. It is advisable to hold staff meetings before leaving the building, so that what is known can be communicated. Use of key communicators in the community will help to convey accurate information. Frequent updates should be made to the public through the media.

Centre for Research Learning and Teaching (2015) in the University of Michigan Study, posited that when conducting Teacher Evaluations, the Evaluation Process should focus attention on Good Teaching Practices to promote a culture in which teaching is highly valued. It is vital that Academic Leaders reassess Evaluation Systems to ensure their reliability, validity, and fairness. There are a variety of methods and settings for Instruction which require various Evaluation Methods and Criteria. Flexibility is a key factor when considering Diversity in Instruction Methods and Academic Leaders will be required to make the following allowances:
- Lectures
- Discussions
- Case Studies
- Field Trips
- Labs
- Small Group Interactions

In addition to the central focus of Classroom Instruction Assessment, the Academic Leader should assess other Teaching Activities, Curriculum Development, New Courses, Classroom Materials, Supervision and Mentoring of Students, and Advising

Students.

The Benefits of Teacher Evaluations are Improvement Purposes and Personnel Decisions. Academic Leaders can provide important evaluative information through Classroom Visits. The focus should be centred on the Appropriateness of Materials and Methods, Breadth and Depth of Materials covered, Relation of Material to the Curricula and Goals of the Course, and Incorporation of Recent Developments in the Discipline. Evaluations provide an informed Appraisal of the Mastery of Content of the Instructor. A Standardized Observation Form will yield systematic and comparable data. A Review of the Curricula, related Course Materials, and Teacher Discussions relating to Lesson Goals and Objectives, prior to the Classroom Observation Visit will enhance the Evaluation Process. There is need to reward and recognize Teaching adequately and find ways to include it in the Evaluation Process. The Instructional Contribution of a Teacher can be evaluated as a value-added element of teaching-related activities, such as, Curriculum Development, Articles submitted to Professional Journals, and other Publication and Authorship of Textbooks and other Instructional Materials.

USING OBSERVATIONS TO IMPROVE QUALITY INSTRUCTION

Bredson (n.d.) stated that Observation of Teachers and teaching in the classroom plays a crucial role in supporting Professional Growth and Development of Teachers. In discussing the principles underlying Classroom Observation, the focus is on the Teacher and the Student. One of the primary tasks of the Principal is to create and maintain positive, healthy teaching and learning environments for everyone in the school, including the Professional Staff. School

Leaders should connect Teacher Learning and Growth to Student Learning and Development. This connection will enrich the ambiance of the School – making it a place of fun, energy, and excitement. It is important for School Leaders to put their professional knowledge into action to create, support, and improve the learning environment in their School.

The School Administration should strive to do everything to put the Teacher at ease and to reduce any anxiety in this unnatural setting of Classroom Observation. Students do become accustomed to the 'outsider' after the first or second visit. It is also advisable for note-taking to be kept to a minimum during the visit, so that there can be maximum concentration on what is being done and said in the lesson. Time should be made available to record Classroom Observations, immediately after the lesson.

It is important for School Leaders to use a variety of activities, according to Bredson (n.d.), to encourage and celebrate learning, such as, personal expressions of congratulations through daily interactions with Teachers and Students. As Teachers explore their pedagogical skills, they need to be assured that the School Leaders will be there to provide professional, emotional, and psychological support in the following areas:
- Teaching and Learning
- Motivation
- Use of Technology

FEEDBACK TO TEACHERS

Feedback is a meaningful activity for many teachers. Highly

effective Principals work to move teachers toward greater levels of independence and professional autonomy by providing feedback on Quality of Instruction, in the following ways:
- Quality vs Quantity
- Modelling
- Slowing Down

It is vital that Principals understand the characteristics of meaningful feedback, such as making suggestions. This Feedback will help Teachers address the challenges they face in their class and will give Teachers discretion and choice on how to follow up on those suggestions.

Feedback tends to work best in the following situations:
- Provided within 24 hours of the Classroom Observation
- Engaged in two-way discussions
- Based on careful and systematic documentation
- Based on factual data and agreed criteria
- Leads to professional growth and development

It is highly recommended that verbal feedback should be given soon after the Observation, highlighting key points only. Written Feedback must be shared with the Teacher within 48 hours of the Observation, to ensure that the experience is still 'fresh'. The Written Feedback must be retained both by the School and the Teacher.

Teachers need to be given the opportunity to express themselves and reflect on their strengths and weaknesses in Post-Observation Conference Meetings. Teachers should be encouraged not to accept what is set forth in the Post-Observation Conference Meeting as a way not to risk their jobs, but rather should consider the

Observation Process as one that adds to their Professional Growth and Development.

To alleviate what may be potential concerns in the lesson, it is important that the Observer begins with positive comments by complimenting the Teacher on particular aspects that have been observed with the desire to give professional support to the Teacher. An 'open' climate should be created which sets a foundation for positive outcomes and decisions, in order to minimize tension in the classroom, and between Teacher and the Observer. Effective School Leaders improve teaching and learning and initiate discussions about Instructional Approaches used in the classrooms, such as, individual, small group, and whole group. The learning-focused School Leadership Team is intent on helping Teachers improve their Practice.

The purpose of the Classroom Visit should be to support development rather than monitor, evaluate, or ensure compliance. In order to reduce defensiveness, Teachers need to have a clear focus about the purpose of Classroom Visits. Being observed can be the most nerve-racking experience, even for the most seasoned Teacher. Teachers often resent the Observation Process because they perceive Principals and other Observers as passing judgment and verdicts on their teaching practices. It is vital that Teachers view Classroom Observation as a culture of collaboration, acceptance, and constructive criticism, rather a judgmental approach. Classroom Observation is an integral part of teaching and learning and allows the Observer to make careful scrutiny of Instruction, Teaching Styles, Classroom Management, and Interactions.

Observations have the tendency to be associated with a 'climate of fear' and Teachers become resistant in engaging in the experience. It is, therefore, necessary for the School Administration to develop the specific skills to fundamentally reduce the impact Observations have on Professional Development. The Observer needs to establish a climate of trust at the outset in the Pre-Observation Conference Meeting to discuss the following matters:

- The context of the Lesson
- Time and place of the Observation
- Where to be positioned in the Classroom
- How to interact with the Students, and
- How long the visit should be

At the start of the Meeting, a good observer will ask the Teacher to comment on their feelings about the Lesson. Observers should endeavor to provide honest, constructive Feedback. The aim of the Observer is for Teachers to accept criticism, professionally and objectively.

Once there is an established style that the School Leader and the Teacher are comfortable with, the initial meeting time can be reduced. A strong collaboration between the School Leader and the Teacher will not only benefit the Teacher, but the School Leader, as well. Gaining the confidence of Teachers will lead to a professional environment; Teachers and Principals working towards sharing a common goal by improving Student Outcomes, their own Professional Development, and the overall image of the School.

LEADERSHIP REFLECTION

Discuss THREE Ways that your Evaluation Process encourages

Professional Growth and Learning

_____
_____
_____
_____
_____
_____
_____
_____
_____
_____
_____

School Administrators can meet individually with Teachers to plan the Classroom Visit Schedule. They both can collaborate to identify a certain area of skillful teaching on which to target. The Administrator can now view the lesson through a particular analytical lens.

LEADERSHIP REFLECTION

Create a Classroom Observation Checklist with SIX guidelines. The Checklist should address the following areas of focus to be utilized in three separate Classroom Visits:
- Lesson Planning for Small Group Instruction
- Student Engagement
- Classroom Management

_____
_____
_____

_____
_____
_____
_____
_____
_____
_____
_____
_____
_____
_____
_____
_____

In your Follow-Up Meeting with a Teacher, after the Post-Conference Meeting, provide examples of:
- ONE Positive Comment
- ONE Prompt, Question, or Suggestion

_____
_____
_____
_____

For an effective Class Observation System, it is essential to have trained Evaluators who spend more time with their Teachers to discuss Performance and Improve Teaching and Learning.

Let us reflect for a moment on a typical Teacher Observation Process in the 20th Century.

Scenario 1

During an academic year, one Classroom Observation Visit was announced which means that the Goal Setting Process was demonstrated. The Classroom Visit lasted approximately 30 – 40 minutes. There would be a Meeting with the Principal in his Office to have formal conversation, after the Observation. Teachers can recall that many times those Observations resulted in receiving very little Feedback.

Let us now examine a typical Teacher Observation Process in the 21st Century.

Scenario 2

Today, unannounced observations have also become popular. This Process seeks to observe Teachers and Students in their natural environment. Principals conduct their Walkthroughs and stay for some length of time, and then the Teacher receive an Evaluation from the Observer outlining what was observed during the Process.

EVALUATING LESSON PLANS

Teachers should be encouraged to evaluate their Lesson Plans. It does not have to be exhaustive to be effective. It does not need to anticipate all possible questions, responses, and comments. The Lesson Plan provides a general outline of Teaching Goals, Learning Objectives, and the means to accomplish them. It should clearly state what is to be done and how it is to be done. The Learning Community is created by Teachers and Students whereby they learn from each other.

Take a few minutes to reflect on the effectiveness of your teaching. A number of extraneous circumstances can prevent the effectiveness of a Lesson Plan. Teachers should be encouraged to reflect on their Lesson Plans a few minutes after each class to assess what worked well and why, and what could have been done differently. Identifying effective and less effective Class Time Management, will allow the Teacher to seek to adjust to the Contingencies of the Classroom.

CRITERIA FOR TEACHER EVALUATION

CRITERIA FOR TEACHER EVALUATION	WHAT TO LOOK FOR?
DETERMINE LEARNING OUTCOMES	What are the most important Concepts, Skills, and Ideas the Teacher wants the Students to grasp? Why are these Concepts important?
INTRODUCTION AND LESSON DEVELOPMENT	How did the Teacher check for the prior knowledge of Students? Are there any possible misconceptions that the Students may be familiar with? How was the Topic introduced?
PLAN LEARNING ACTIVITIES TO ATTRACT STUDENT ATTENTION	How did the Teacher explain the Topic? How were the Students engaged? What were the relevant Real-life Examples utilized to support Students through the Lesson? What Methods or Strategies were utilized to help Students have a

	better understanding of the Topic?
CHECK FOR STUDENT UNDERSTANDING	What Questioning Techniques were utilized to check for understanding of the Lesson? How did the Students demonstrate their understanding of the Lesson? Did the Teacher check the Objectives that were accomplished against the activities designed for each listed Objective?
DEVELOP CONCLUSION AND PREVIEW	Did the Teacher summarize the main points of the Lesson? - Teacher-lead - Student-directed - Whole-class written statements Did the Teacher explain any ambiguous interpretations? Was there a preview for the next Lesson to help them to connect with the ideas within a larger context?
PRESENT REALISTIC TIMELINES	Did the Teacher estimate the duration of activities by indicating the time allotted to each activity? How did the Teacher plan for time at the end of the Lesson? - Questions - Summary - Extra Work in case time remains - Flexibility according to the needs of the Students

Academic Leaders usually have a record of demonstrated effectiveness in their own classrooms and are Instructional Experts.

The Principal will benefit from increasing the capacity of the Leadership Team. Vice Principals and Department Heads are in an excellent position to provide quality Feedback to Teachers.

It is vital for Principals to assess the needs of the School to determine when it is necessary to adjust their focus to build capacity on high-quality Feedback rather than increasing the number of Observations. Academic Leaders can be deployed within the School Building to help observe and coach new Teachers. Regular discussions with Academic Leaders on high-quality Feedback will enhance the skill required to Conduct Evaluations.

According to the Education First (2015), Teachers can realize and reach their potential with Evaluation Systems that include Feedback that is high-quality and actionable. Systems can be improved and sustained overtime when Teachers are provided with Feedback and Support. Teachers will value and support Evaluation Systems, if they consistently receive Feedback that helps improve their Instruction. The quality Feedback and Support provided to Teachers appear to be making significant impact on Instructional Improvement and positive growth in Student Outcomes.

School Leadership should focus on regular, ongoing Feedback to support Teachers in improving their Performance Levels. Today, time and resources are invested in raising the bar for School Leaders to know Good Teaching, identify areas of strengths, areas of growth, and ongoing communication on ways to hone their craft. Evaluators are expected to be involved in Ongoing Professional Learning which focuses on a common set of standards.
Principals can provide a script for Academic Leaders involved in the Evaluation Process. Scripts facilitate the Feedback Conversation in

the Post-Observation Conference. Fewer surprises in the Evaluation Process are expected when Principals adopt Transparent Scripts, Samples, and Templates.

COLLABORATIVE PROGRAMME DELIVERY

School Leaders should seek to explore all avenues to strengthen Collaboration with their Teachers. Collaborative Planning and ongoing Professional Dialogue about Teaching and Learning represent various Delivery Strategies for meeting the needs of Teachers. Programme Delivery Teams include those Professionals involved in Programming, Planning, and Designing Leadership Roles for the Programme. The Team Members can support each other in goal setting and examining connections between their own Learning and Student Learning. Collaboration will improve the professional craft which is crucial to School Improvement and Student Success.

Assembling an effective Team is critical to achieving the best outcomes possible. The Team will consist of Professional Disciplines and Technical Specialists. Opportunities are created for Team Members to demonstrate high levels of trust; personal satisfaction; increased collaboration; shared risk and reward; and open exchange of information.

The Collaborative Approach fosters Innovation, Synergistic Gain, and Programme Enhancement by offering ways of delivering more Programmes in less time and less resources. Interactions can lead to mutual benefits, whereby reusable learning is utilized, such as, effective procedures and methods, enhanced interests, and capacities of others.

Collaborative Programme Delivery is characterized by a Team Building mode based upon Trust with the 4 Cs: A Sense of Common Purpose, Commitment, Community Involvement, and Cooperation. In order to achieve success, there has to be willingness to work together to achieve collective purpose. The Team works toward a common agenda and potentially capable of generating and pursuing collective strategies which will result in added value, flexibility, and innovation. The Collaborative Model involves tension when operating in a severely constrained resource environment, where organizations survive on self-interest.

Collaborative Strategies can promote reflection and include the following:
- Making Suggestions
- Giving Feedback
- Modelling
- Utilizing Inquiry
- Soliciting Advice and Opinions
- Giving Praise

Effective School Leaders serve as Mentors and Coaches which can yield positive effects on Teacher and Student Motivation. It is paramount that Administrators foster ongoing positive interactions with Students and engage Teachers in thoughtful, purposeful, appropriate, and non-threatening Dialogue in the following ways:
- Listening
- Using examples and demonstrations
- Allowing Teachers and Students to make choices
- Sharing their experiences
- Offering Professional Guidance and Literature

- Recognizing the strengths of Teachers and Students
- Maintaining focus on improved Instruction

The Learning Community will benefit from the Collaboration Dialogue because it will build the confidence level of Teachers, help them to learn more about their teaching, encourage them to continue to utilize various Learning Styles, and provide opportunities for risk-taking in the Classroom. Effective Schools have Instructional Leaders who value dialogue that encourages Teachers to critically reflect on their Learning and Professional Practice. In addition to working with Teachers collaboratively, Instructional Leaders need to be able to speak convincingly about what they observe in the Classroom, if they are to support Teaching and Learning. Highly Effective Instructional Leaders are involved in Modelling, Coaching, Facilitating, but are not Governors of Learning. Analyzing Instruction and Diagnosing Growth Needs of Teachers are necessary skills for Instructional Leader.

There is motivation for Cooperative Relationships to emerge and operate effectively for institutions aspiring to be involved in Capacity Building. It is important for the Team to harness contributions from the Community which allows for a broader sense of ownership. Getting to know key individuals and building relationships in the School environment, sometimes take a lot of time, but once Administrators and Teachers are Committed, it will lead to sustained relationships over time. Additional benefits gained by Teams working together offer Schools the opportunity to have improved delivery of Objectives and create new ones. Building Capacity in the School has the potential to create, nurture, and maintain overtime an effective self-renewing and authentic Learning Community.

LEADERSHIP REFLECTION

Create a School Environment in which Teachers have access to the support they need

___

Examine the Role of the School Leader in supporting Teachers by creating Collaborative School Environments

___

TEAM BUILDING – POSITIVE DEPARTMENTAL CULTURE

Human motivations and needs are so complex and creating a positive School Climate can assist in providing solutions to classroom and whole-school challenges.

Let us take a moment to visualize a Positive Departmental Culture. There is an immediate feeling of the Department Culture as soon as the following social and professional interactions among individuals in the Department are observed:
- Is there harmony demonstrated by the Students, Teachers, and School Leaders?
- Are the Members of the Department treating each other with respect?
- Is the Physical Surrounding clean and orderly?
- Are the Display/Bulletin Boards sending a positive message?

- Are Students engaged in Learning?

It is vital that School Leaders utilize every opportunity to be proven trustworthy by listening to the voices of Teachers, Students, Parents, and Community Members; involving all in the Decision-making Process; and facilitating Trust-building among Stakeholders. To ensure that there is little or no bias in assessing the School Climate, an independent third party should conduct individual Interviews.

A Shared Vision should emerge from Personal Vision. The values, concerns, and aspirations are beliefs and represent Personal Visions. School Leaders should create a positive climate in Schools whereby Students, Teachers, Parents, and Community Members feel comfortable sharing their ideas. When individuals work together to create a Shared Vision, it increases the likelihood for the Vision to be carried out.

LEADERSHIP REFLECTION

CASE STUDY 1 – DEPARTMENTAL CULTURE
The Departmental Culture that Clara Jones worked in was not one that encouraged seeking advice or support. There was little or no exchange among colleagues at the School or Department, to the point where Clara felt that when she asked questions, she was disturbing her colleagues. Whenever challenging situations surfaced, Clara would seek the support of her Principal and was told she needs to arrive at a solution on her own. Clara had very limited experience in Classroom Management and Developing Effective Lessons, even after four years at the School.
Clara had a very different experience when she moved to another

School, two years later. The Principal and Staff were supportive and welcomed her questions. Clara felt comfortable asking for support and rose to a level where she began taking risks. The respect she received as a Teacher, gave her confidence in her ability to teach and she was able to celebrate with her Students, as they made greater academic achievements than at the previous School.

Explain TWO Ways that Administrators can cultivate Positive Relationships with Teachers that will contribute to an overall effective School Environment for all, citing appropriate examples from the Case Study.

___

CASE STUDY 2 – INSTRUCTIONAL SUPERVISION: LESSON PLANNING

One major challenge being experienced by Riverside Primary School in the area of Instructional Supervision is the lack of planning by Teachers. Miss Morgan, a Teacher with six years of teaching experience is usually unprepared for her Lessons. The Principal, Mr. Jenkins, made the following Observations during a Lesson:

- Lesson was Teacher-centred
- Hands-on activities for Students were limited
- Resource Material was inadequate
- Lesson was not sequentially developed
- When questioned by Mr. Jenkins, she offered no reason for the lack of preparation and failure to provide effective learning experiences for Students. Miss Morgan intended, however, that the lesson was to be a review.

How should the Lesson Planning be monitored?

_____
_____
_____
_____
_____
_____
_____

Does lack of adequate planning accurately reflect the level of commitment that Miss Morgan has to education? Give reasons.

_____
_____
_____
_____
_____
_____
_____

How could Teachers be encouraged to seek and prepare Instructional Resource Materials?

To what degree are Student-centred Methods appropriate for our Teaching Environment?

What incentives could be offered to teachers to utilize student-centred methods?

INCORPORATING THE USE OF TECHNOLOGY AND e-LEARNING IN PROGRAMME DELIVERY

Technological Change occurs frequently and drives Student Expectations. The use of Information Technology is observed in the transformation of how Student Grades are recorded and managed and how Educators are trained for specific jobs. There is a need to create and support Schools in Life-long Learning. Flexible Digital Tools are available through easy online access, which enable Teachers to incorporate Technology in their Lessons. Today, the Classrooms benefit from unique computer-aided Programme Delivery which is very appealing to some individuals, because it offers flexibility in how to receive and engage with Course Material, pace the Course Material Delivery, and apply the Technology-designed Material to the Course Content developed to meet the needs of individual Students. Web Pages, containing structured

Materials with further Reading Prompts, Activities, and Tasks, also help to guide the Students.

The Distance Learning Programmes are ideal for individuals who are unable to take the time away from their work base, to attend a Traditional Programme. Online-based Programmes enable employers to be far more flexible in the way they assign individuals their study time. Students require a minimum hardware specification to access e-Learning Material, communicate, and exchange information, which prescribes that Students have sufficient basic skills and knowledge to use a personal computer.
One of the benefits of incorporating Technology in Programme Delivery is that Students are continuously developing and fine-tuning their IT Skills which contribute to work effectiveness and efficiency. Strong Teacher Support is essential when Technology is incorporated into the Lesson. It is important that Students are provided with a point of contact, advice on academic assessments, and feedback on assignments, examinations, and projects by their Teachers.

Administrators need to support Teachers in providing various activities to suit the Learning Styles of Students, create engaging and interactive Lessons, and provide Enrichment Programmes to talented Learners. Students develop and maintain Professional Enabling Skills when they participate in Library Searches, but must be encouraged to utilize their time wisely. It is important for Teachers to remind Students to demonstrate efficient use of their time and limit their Searches and Online Usage to matters directly relevant to completing the Programme.

LEADERSHIP REFLECTION

In your view, discuss whether there should be a restriction of how much of the Learning Material is presented Online and how much directed or non-directed Online Research the Student should receive.

_____
_____
_____
_____
_____
_____
_____
_____
_____
_____
_____
_____
_____

What does Engaging Instruction look like?
Intellectual

_____
_____
_____

Emotional

_____
_____
_____

Behavioural

_____
_____
_____

Social

_____
_____
_____

Ryan (2014) argued that Schools are still struggling and deciding on the best ways to engage Students in effective Teaching and Learning Programmes. The Study indicated that e-Learning contributed to the overall knowledge and skill development of Students. The confidence that Students demonstrate in Technology alone, is instrumental in their workforce preparation, improved method and medium of communication, and teamwork and organization skills.

A repertoire of skills and ability levels are needed if Students are to survive as citizens in the 21st Century, knowledge-based economy. Students who acquire these skills have greater thinking and problem-solving abilities, more self-motivated, larger cooperative interaction capacity, varied specialized skills, and are more resourceful and adaptable, than in previous years. Although Teachers are crucial in the entire process of ensuring that Students are equipped with Online Education, not many Teachers are confident to explore more, and therefore need individualized guidance to assist.

3
PLANNING MEETINGS AND COMMUNICATING IN A TECHNOLOGY-BASED SOCIETY

A Meeting should be conducted when there is a need by a Group or Team to review information, make decisions, or disseminate information. Meetings will normally be successful when there is a clear sense of purpose and effectively managed. Meetings are conducted for the following purposes:

- Exchanging Information and Ideas
- Solving Problems
- Making Decisions
- Reviewing Information
- Gathering Data

Prescott (2011) suggested that Effective Meetings constitute Good Planning, a Highly-skilled Chairperson, and a Follow-up Plan. It is of utmost importance that School Leaders are trained in facilitating Meetings and how to delegate responsibilities to Staff Members. It requires great skill and motivation to get Teachers to conduct High-quality Meetings in a limited timeframe. Most importantly, Meetings should be conducted with an Agenda, so that Participants can follow the process. Teachers should be given the opportunity to submit Agenda Items, prior to the Meeting, as it enhances collaboration and fosters sharing.

FORMS OF MEETINGS

Regular or Standing Committees can be called for ongoing business and operates throughout the life of the organization, such as, Occupational Health and Safety

Inaugural Meetings are held only once for the Commencement of an organization

Annual General Meetings are held once a year to report on the position of the organization to its members or shareholders and to ratify critical decisions

Board Meetings are conducted regularly for normal business transactions

Specific Interest Groups may involve individuals from various sectors, such as, Environmental Awareness Groups

Ad hoc is a group formed for a specific purpose and meets regularly until task is accomplished

Topical Meetings focuses on narrowly defined current issues relating to a particular topic

Department Meetings are conducted regularly to transact business of specific interest

Conferences are held to receive information, consultation, and discussion

Video Conferences allow groups to use Technology to conduct a conference without having to move to a single location

Teleconferences are Business Meetings or Educational Sessions held by groups in different locations involving Telecommunication Equipment

Online Meetings allow groups to carry on business over an electronic medium

Special or Emergency Meetings held when a group needs to address business which require urgent attention and cannot wait until the next Regular Meeting

Seminars and Workshops are groups of individuals who meet to achieve common goals on a study or research area

CODES OF CONDUCT

It is important to provide guidance as it relates to the expectations and behaviour of the Members of the Group or Team. Effective Meetings should have established agreed-upon Rules of interaction. The Rules need to be outlined to the Team Members which will clearly identify acceptable and unacceptable behaviour. Each Member should be encouraged to serve as active partners in decision-making. Once the groundwork is laid, it increases the likelihood of positive outcomes. Ground Rules may include Confidentiality; Respect; Participation; No Distractions; and Punctuality.

It is important that Ground Rules are communicated prior to

Teleconferences, Video Conferences, and Online Meetings, and Meeting Reminders are circulated. These Rules include Introduction of Participants and a decision made as to whom and when each Member will speak should be established at the beginning of the Meeting. Names should be used when addressing others. Telephones and other electronic devices should be muted. For Video Conferences, eye contact should be made with the Camera. Ensure that all electronic communication connections function properly and Group Members practice using the Software, prior to the Meeting.

PLANNING THE MEETING

Send an e-mail out two weeks before the Meeting reminding the committee about the Meeting and ask for Agenda items.
Verify the Location of the meeting ensuring it is appropriate for the number of people you expect as well as any Technology you need and space for Food/Refreshments.

Have the Agenda, any attachments, and the Minutes from the previous Meeting out to the committee a week before the Meeting.
If there is something particularly critical that the committee needs to know prior to the Meeting, include it in the text of the e-mail that contains the above attachments.

Make sure there are copies of the Agenda, Minutes and any Handouts available at the Meeting.

Check with the Secretary of the committee to know who has sent their regrets or may be arriving late, and adjust the Agenda accordingly.

Take your copy of the Agenda and make whatever notes you need that will help you remember what are essential, so as not to forget during the Meeting.

Members should be reminded of any task that needs their attention prior to the next Meeting.

LEADERSHIP REFLECTION

Produce a List of ITEMS FOR CODE OF CONDUCT Consideration

_____
_____
_____
_____
_____
_____
_____
_____
_____
_____
_____
_____
_____

Discuss the Importance for Consensus for Decisions in Meetings

_____
_____
_____
_____
_____
_____

_____
_____
_____
_____
_____

ROLES OF TEAM MEMBERS

Specific Meeting Roles and Responsibilities should be defined. The Leader is responsible for guiding the Team to accomplishing its mission. Other Team Members may be responsible for guiding particular aspects of the Meeting. During the Meeting, the Group or Team may require various Administrative Supports, such as, Recording Information, Documenting the Agenda, Time-keeping, and Preparing Reports.

The Group Members have responsibilities prior to the Meeting, during the Meeting, and after the Meeting. Preparing for the Meeting is a requirement for Group Members which involves conducting a research on Agenda Items. A Review of the Agenda ensures that each Member is prepared with necessary information. For a Meeting to achieve its goals, it is paramount that Group Members maximize their Participation, remain focused, and support the decisions of others. During the Meeting, Group Members should expect to contribute their ideas by Speaking; Listening, Cooperating; Sharing Information; Dedicating and Concentrating of Efforts; and Focusing on a Common Goal. Action is required after the Meeting, which may involve implementing a solution or supporting a function. Evaluating the Outcomes against the Objectives of the Meeting should be performed as part of the Follow-up Procedures, after the Meeting. Follow-up

Strategies are established in order to keep the momentum after the Meeting, which include, distributing Meeting Minutes and updating Participants who were unable to attend the Meeting. It is vital to monitor the completion of the Action Items.

DEVELOPING THE AGENDA

Start with the Minutes from the last Meeting and ensure that the Agenda has items that are needed that either are a result of the last Meeting or are a continuation from that Meeting.

Always start with Welcome and Introductions even if there are no new Members.

Depending on the type of committee, ensure that the next items are Adoption of the Agenda and Approval/Business Arising from the Minutes of the last Meeting.

If you have asked your committee ahead of for Agenda items, do not include an "Other" item at the end, but do end your Agenda with the next Meeting date. You can also include subsequent Meeting dates if they are known.

Take some time to determine how many items on the Agenda will be mostly just information sharing, produce a discussion, and/or need a decision.

Simultaneously, knowing the length of your Meeting, decide if you can cover all items on the Agenda and create the Agenda accordingly. If you know you have too many items given the time, place the least urgent items at the end of the Agenda and let the committee know as such.

When developing the order of the Agenda, keep in mind if any Member will be arriving late or will need to leave early.

If there are Guests attending the Meeting to present an item, it is always better to place their items at the start of the Agenda so they can leave once their item is complete.

If all else is equal, place the most important items, especially those that will require a lengthy discussion and/or decision, at the top of the Agenda.

Leave items that are mostly information until the end of the Agenda.

Where applicable, put the name of the person who will be addressing each item and, if it is a timed item, put the time that the item will be addressed.

New Business refers to any item not covered by the Agenda and a Member would like to have it discussed

CONTENTS OF THE AGENDA

- Purpose of the Meeting
- Objectives of the Meeting
- Topic for Discussion
- Presenter or Discussion Leader for each Topic
- Time Allotment for each Topic

The Participants should be carefully selected to attend the Meeting.

Individuals with the authority to make certain decisions and those with the relevant skill set should be on the Team. Quality discussions should be encouraged, which can only be achieved when the right Members are invited to attend and for productive participation. Team Members should be informed of any Leader Roles to be assumed, such as, Presentations. Invitations may be sent via Email or Calendar Invite. Attendees may be asked to submit their Agenda Items and then a Final Agenda sent to all Meeting Participants before the Meeting.

A convenient and accessible location should be selected. The Size of the Meeting will dictate the configuration design, such as, Roundtable or U-Shape. Other Logistic Considerations may include Refreshments, Catering, Noise Reduction, Room Temperature, Seating Arrangements, Lighting, Smell, Colour, and Audio-Visual Aids.

Choosing a time for the Meeting is crucial. The Meeting Time should be convenient and possible for most Participants. Starting on Time allows for the List Items on the Agenda to be completed.

STEPS IN CONDUCTING A MEETING

- Start on Time
- Communicate the Purpose of the Meeting to Participants
- Assign Meeting Roles
- Have individuals knowledgeable in the Policies and Procedures being discussed agree on Ground Rules and Procedures
- Follow the Agenda and Document the Decisions
- End on Time

CREATING SCHOOL "BASE TEAMS"

Staff Members are assigned to Base Teams which are long-term and heterogeneous. Staff Members are involved at the beginning and end of the Meeting. Meetings are kept at a personalized level and are School-wide focused. Peer Support is provided in an effort to celebrate staff efforts. Staff Members are expected to be active participants in the Meeting.

Base Teams promote pair work with a recommended four on each Team. Teams can be assigned by random selection or a combination of grades, subjects, areas, or experience. Team Members are rotated every six to ten months. The Teams summarize the proceedings at the end of each Meeting.

LEADERSHIP REFLECTION

Visualize a Meeting you will be having in the near future.
With a Partner:

Plan your Purpose

_____
_____
_____
_____

Establish your Objective(s)

_____
_____
_____

Create an Agenda

_____
_____
_____
_____
_____
_____
_____
_____
_____

MOCK MEETING ACTIVITY

- Set up Table Groups
- Select one Group Member to lead Mock Meeting
- Leader will use the Agenda
- Team Members will select a skill
- Presentation should demonstrate the accomplishment of the Meeting Goals

TIME MANAGEMENT

Bizmove (n.d.) stated that Time Management is one of the most difficult facilitation tasks. Keeping track of time is vital for Effective Meetings. If the Meeting is running behind schedule, present the Item for Discussion to the Group, asking for the input of the Team.

FACTORS THAT DERAIL MEETINGS

Group Members should be encouraged to be punctual for Meetings. Starting late penalizes members who were on time for the Meeting.

Shorter Meetings are favoured by Participants and can be achieved by sticking to the Agenda. Clearly establishing the Meeting Purpose will promote Productive Meetings. In order to add variety, the use of film clips can be used to generate discussions and also inviting a speaker.

OBSERVING PROTOCOLS

Bizmove (n.d.) highlighted Protocols to be observed in Meetings. Participants should be notified of the Meeting Date, well in advance and provided with an Agenda and Background Data. Arrangements with Resource Personnel should be confirmed prior to the Meeting. It is protocol to introduce guests and newcomers at the beginning. Expressing gratitude to Team Members and Individuals outside the group for significant contributions to the success of the Meeting is a common courtesy of Meetings. In situations of Postponement or Cancellations, invitees should be advised as far in advance as possible. Unless Protocol would have it different, list Participants in alphabetical order in Meeting Announcements and Minutes.

PHYSICAL SETTING

Attention should be placed on the Physical Setting of the Meeting. The Convenience of the Location should be taken into consideration, as well as, the Size of the Room, Seating Arrangements and Availability of Extra Seats, Lighting, Heating, Ventilation, any Visual Aids required and their proper use, and Name Tags, if necessary.

It is important to take the following points into consideration when Planning the Location:

Choose a Venue for the Meeting based on the size of the Team and where the Members of your Team live and work.

Make sure that the Location is clearly indicated on the Agenda along with any special instructions for parking, a need to sign in for some buildings, or which door to enter by.
Within the Location, ensure that there are bathrooms nearby and that there is a convenient Location within the room for Food/Refreshments.

If this Team meets on a regular basis, try to find a Location that can be used for every Meeting so Team Members are accustomed.
Assuming these are Meetings where Team Members need to refer to documents and you want productive discussions to occur, choose a room that gives everyone enough space for their documents and allows good eye contact amongst all Team Members.

If the number attending the Meeting is going to be larger or smaller than normal, consider an alternate Location within that same building if possible. It is always best to have the space be a good fit for the number of Members attending.

If you need access to Technology, ensure that the necessary equipment is present and in good working order. Ideally, you are able to test that equipment ahead of time to ensure it is working.

PARTICIPATION AND ATTENDANCE

According to Bizmove (n.d.), participants should be viewed as Management Resources and invited to make contributions to

Meetings in the form of knowledge and/or experience. It is important that invitations be issued to interested individuals so as not to impede the Meeting.

When Meetings exceed seven, it allows for more centralized communication and less opportunities for direct interaction; the predicted outcome gets more difficult as the number of Participants increase. Larger Meetings are more formal and there may be need for extra time to cover each Topic.

The "Small Group" Theory referred to by Bizmove (n.d.), considers seven to be the maximum number of Participants for a Productive Meeting. A Meeting exceeding 18 Participants may suffer from unaccomplished Meeting Objectives. On the other hand, if Meetings have less than three individuals in attendance, there can be situations where two Participants support each other and the ideas of the third Participant are unheard, which can result in non-productivity.

ROBERT RULES ORDER

Meetings should resort to Robert Rules when Attendance is too large or discussions become heated. The Chairman is called upon to Manage the Meeting, Speak when appropriate, Encourage Discussion, Seek Consensus, and Summarize. The Chairman is not allowed to "hog" the discussion, play the comic, chastise other Participants, or let the Meeting run by itself.

When Chairing a Meeting, the Chairman should:

- Where possible, always start your Meeting on time and end on time as Team Members will respect that you are mindful of the time they are giving.
- Ensure there is someone to take Minutes.
- Begin each Meeting with a warm welcome and have each Member introduce themselves, if there are any new Members.
- If there are guests attending the Meeting, make sure they are aware that they may leave the meeting once their item on the Agenda has been completed. If there are items on the Agenda of a confidential nature, then you need to ensure that Guests exit after their item.
- Ensure that each Member has an Agenda, Minutes, and a copy of any other document needed for the Meeting.
- Review the Agenda to remind Members of which items are of more importance and also remind individuals of when the Meeting should end.
- As you work through the Agenda, be mindful of the end time as you should have an approximate idea of how long each item should take.
- With each item, be aware of which items need to come to a conclusion or can be extended to the next Meeting.
- If there are items that need a decision, balance the time it takes to give individuals a chance to voice their opinion and ask questions. When it is felt that all meaningful input has been given, ask one more time for any clarifications and then proceed to the vote or general acceptance, if you are using consensus as your decision-making tool.
- If the discussion of an item is not finding its own way to a logical conclusion, suggest to the Team that this item can be tabled and addressed at the next Meeting. Make it clear to

the Team what additional information may be needed before being able to solve this item.
- At the conclusion of the Meeting, remind Team Members of the decisions taken at the Meeting that are 'going forward' items as well as any homework they have between now and the next Meeting. Lastly, make sure they are aware of when the next Meeting is.

School Administrators in the 21st Century need to conduct High-quality Meetings that promote the following features:
- Protocols
- Skills
- Behaviours
- Practice

Teachers should be taught how to value Staff Meetings and be active participants in the process.

Let us take into consideration that Teachers should be treated no different from Students, to some extent. Understanding the Learning Styles of each Participant in the Meeting is the responsibility of the School Administrator. Visual Learners may want to view the proceedings, by way of the Agenda, prior to and during the Meeting. Kinesthetic Learners may be interested in the time allotted for the Meeting.

LEADERSHIP REFLECTION

Discuss THREE Ways in which you can improve your Leadership Team Meetings to make them more effective and Leadership-focused.

Your School has appointed a New Principal. As Department Head you were invited to a Meeting and surprised that the Meeting atmosphere was different. The room was arranged with Tables with four Chairs at each. Refreshments were placed at a Table located towards the side of the room. Strategically placed on a wall in front of the room was a Poster entitled "Meeting Ground Rules." Participants were allowed a few minutes to share in Refreshments and engage in 'meet and greet' activities. The Meeting started promptly with a quick review of the Agenda followed by Team Building Activities at each Table. There was a stimulating and productive experience at the end of the Meeting which combined small- and large-group Activities focusing on the ways to Incorporate Technology in achieving goals in various subject areas.

Comment on how this Meeting could be used by your new School Principal to change the focus from Information Transmission to Relationship Building, Professional Development, Problem-Solving, and Decision-Making.

_____
_____
_____
_____
_____
_____
_____
_____
_____
_____
_____
_____

Discuss the value of establishing agreed-upon Norms of Expected Behaviour at the first Staff Meeting for the School Year

_____
_____
_____
_____
_____
_____
_____
_____
_____
_____

From the List provided, Contribute THREE possible Group Norm Agreements:

We will begin the Meeting on Time

We will conduct the Meeting from a Staff-developed Agenda

___

Develop a Follow-up Plan for a Meeting that you conducted in your School

___

Staff Members who have been affected, have complained to you about concerns that they have with the Principal of your Institution, and he does not appear to value the Employees.

As the Teachers' Association Representative for your Educational Context, how would you seek to address this Conflict?

4
STRATEGIC PLANNING IN AN EDUCATIONAL COMMUNITY

The Purpose of Planning, as defined by the California State Department of Finance (1998), is the improved opportunity of reaching desirable possible outcomes. Strategic Plans are guidelines that shape an Organization in what it does and why it does it. The authors suggested that this Team effort allows for Collaborative Problem-solving on a future direction for the Organization.

Strategic Planning is evolving in increasingly complex environments; therefore, it is important for Administrators to be proactive. The Requirements of Strategic Planning includes Broad-based Information Collection, Exploration of Alternatives, and Future Implications of Present Decisions. Success involves combined reflective thinking of accurate analysis and innovation. The authors stated that the Strategic Planner exercises wise judgment in Technological Possibilities, and Political and Economic Realities. Fundamental to Good Management is Strategic Planning and Budgeting; the Strategic Plan provides direction, while on the other hand, the Budget provides Resources to implement the Plan (Strategic Planning Guidelines, 1998).

Schools should deploy the Resources in ways that best support the Student Goals and Objectives. Spending Patterns vary considerably between Schools and therefore, the optimal mix will differ. School Leaders not only play a prominent role in Managing the Finances of the School, but also set the direction of the School. Effective

Financial Practices include Managing Resources and Processes so that the Budget is aligned with the Strategic Plan of the School. In larger Schools, Budgeting allows for Delegation of financial responsibilities and tasks.

Consider for a moment: A Strategic Plan without a link to your School Budget, would be a dream. Similarly, a Budget without Strategic Thinking would be demonstrating an unresponsive School Environment. Strategic Planning steers the Budget Process; Planning and Budgeting are interactive.

Today, Schools are required to share their Strategic Plan with Teachers, Students, Parents, Community Members, and other Stakeholders. When there is open relationship between the School Administration and the School Community, it ensures that challenges are met positively, lines of accountability are clear, and decisions can be justified. Strategic Planning is the process of Goal Setting, deciding on actions to achieve those Goals, and mobilizing Resources to meet the stated objectives. Strategic Planning in Education is now shaping into a community-involved process which has resulted in more effective and supported Plans. Community Engagement is an essential element in building a Successful Plan. School Leaders are enjoying the multiple benefits of early and frequent Community Involvement. When School Leaders embrace Teachers, Parents, Students, Community Members, and other Stakeholders, they are inviting them to participate in the Strategic Planning process. Technology has no doubt, played an important role in the ongoing change to the Strategic Planning Process.

School Leaders will need to develop a Strategic Plan that outlines

the direction the Institution will be pursuing. The Plan will reflect the duration for which the Strategies will be pursued with reassessment periods built in. The design of the initial plan will be supported by data which will be analyzed to establish start and end points. Input from the various Stakeholders would be essential to be incorporated in the preliminary planning stages. The role of the School Leadership Team involves conducting frequent and consistent analyses of Data reflecting the following information:
- Student Performance
- Teaching Strategies
- Leadership Practices

Quality Leadership is vital for cultivating a School Culture that focuses on Learning and Achievement for all Students. It is fundamental that the Strategic Plan reflect the belief that School Leadership and Teaching have an effect on Student Outcomes. Schools should utilize the abilities and talents of the Teachers, Students, Parents, and the wider community in building and committing to the Strategic Direction of the School. This collaboration will result in Schools becoming stronger and participants in the decision-making process feeling involved in the School Agenda.

A Primary Task of the School Administrator is monitoring the prior year Scores of Student Achievement. Let us reflect on questions that a School Administrator may ask:
- Is the Programme, Strategy, or Initiative working?
- What Strategies can be employed to improve all areas of the School?
- Is there a relationship between Leadership Practices and Changes in Student Achievement?

- Can effective Teaching Practices be identified?
- How will the Goals be accomplished?
- Are Resources been allocated appropriately?

It is of utmost importance that School Leaders are in one accord, and rather reflect on the process as continuous creation of Plans for Systems, Programmes, Curricula, and Initiatives.

In dealing with Strategic Issues, the 21st Century Instructional Leader should:
- Meet with the Leadership Team prior to the start of the year to identify issues
- Focus on solutions rather than problems
- Pool solutions together
- Articulate a clear vision to Teachers and ensure they embrace the concept of Transformation of the Learning Environment
- Observe and evaluate Instruction
- Re-evaluate Curriculum by involving the Stakeholders based on the relevant skills for the 21st Century
- Promote Professional Development which will transform the Teaching and Learning Culture in Schools

Effective School Leadership Teams use multi-faceted data to provide insights into Student Outcomes to inform decision-making, make enquiries, and identify and prioritize issues and solutions.
Let us examine the following questions that will assist in guiding School Leaders in establishing a Strategic Framework for Analysis, Planning, and Decision-making:
- What evidence would best inform the Leadership Team

- How valid and reliable is the Evidence and Data as a measure of Student Achievement and Engagement
- Is there a proper equilibrium of Qualitative and Quantitative Data

It is important that School Leaders focus on Analysis, and not only on Data. The following processes need to be implemented by the 21st Century Strategic Leader in order to promote shared understanding of Instructional Change and School Improvement:

- Commitment to Student Excellence
- Ongoing Reflective Thinking
- The use of Data to build Collaborative Learning Cultures with Students, Parents, and the School Communities to attain improved Student Achievement
- Use of both Types of Assessments – Formative and Summative – to provide Feedback to Students, Teachers, and Parents
- Willingness to re-allocate Resources to areas that promote effective Student Outcomes
- Shifting Accountability of Leadership Training to Capacity Building
- Strategic Planning that has a clear vision of the Community needs and Global trends will expose students to Curriculum that will potentially prepare them for both the local and the international community. This reflects the qualities of effective Leadership where all the Resources are utilized in such a manner where the plan is designed to meet the present and future needs of the Institution.

A good Strategic Plan can improve Student Outcomes, retain the best Teachers, and enhance School Leadership. An integral part of the Strategic Plan is the Financial Forecast, which should include monetary values for each of the Expenditures outlined in the Strategic Plan matched with Resource Implications of its targets. The Strategic Plan should be affordable and realistic. The Principal has the responsibility to outline the following key developments:

- New Curricula
- Staff Planning Issues
- Student Number Targets
- Building Projects
- Capital Expenditures

Similarly, estimates for Funding are to be reviewed to determine if there are any increases or decreases in Public or Private Funding. It is fundamental that School Leaders understand the key assumptions underlying the Forecast.

Let us examine possible Projections:

- People
- Time
- Money

These most fundamental Priorities support the Instructional Model. Projections represent future financial performance and levels of activity. Built into these figures are varying levels of certainty and confidence. These Financial Projections can be extracted from Departmental-level Budgets by Identifying Trends, Demand Factor, and Strategic Issues which support the Budget Process.

ALIGNING STRATEGY TO BUDGETS

Schools require money for Teachers, Learning Resources, and Facilities, according to The Ministry of Education, Ontario, Ideas into Action, Bulletin 6 (2014), in order to ensure Academic Success for Students. Based on Research, the authors suggested that high-

performing Schools carefully consider the following Strategies to allocate Resources:
- Investing continuously in improving Teaching Quality
- Creating Personal Learning Opportunities
- Maximizing Instructional Time and linking that time to Student Learning

Researchers further concluded that School Leaders, Teachers, and Parents need to identify their highest Priority which would allow them the tools to allocate Resources to support those Priorities. The authors suggested that in advancing Student Achievement and Engagement, there is need for Schools to highlight the following interdependent elements:
- Instructional Systems that inform ongoing Instruction and articulate the "what" and "how"
- Professional Capacity that describes the need for Quality Teaching Staff, Professional Learning, and Social Resources that promote Teamwork and Problem-solving
- Collaboration with Parents, Community, and the School will, by its strength, reap important Resources for the Classroom, and directly lead to Student Motivation
- A Welcoming Learning Environment that fosters a positive Student Outcome
- Dual Leadership Role to drive Student Success which involves Instructional and Collaborative Leadership; the former relates to Establishing Strategic Priorities for Utilizing Resources and Collaborative Leadership, on the other side, Promoting Partnerships among Schools, Teachers, Parents, and Community Members.

Without the link to Budgets, Strategies will run the risk of becoming invisible and may result in the Programme not being adequately resourced. The Budget Process needs focus, hence the need to make connections. Schools can transform Budgeting into a valuable Collaborative Process in which individuals can see the "Big Picture" of how their daily activities affect the School-wide Strategic Initiatives.

The authors of Ministry of Education, Ontario, Ideas into Action, Bulletin 6 (2014) support Reeves (2011) in the Process for Linking Strategy to Budget.

Let us look closer at each Activity:

Establishing Focus

The authors suggested that the common belief for both School Leaders and Teachers is Academic Success for Students. School Leaders will identify a maximum of six Priorities linked to Student Needs, as it relates to Instructional Initiatives. The Strategies to drive Student Success should also be noted, at this stage. Leaders in Education are responsible for Teacher hire, Teacher assignment to classrooms, Teacher retention, and Teacher Quality Improvements, and therefore, should promote challenging Goals that have the greatest effect on Student Outcomes. It is important that School Leaders explore empowering ways to support their focus on Priorities and remove personal assumptions.

Staying on Track

Total commitment to Academic Success, will allow the School Leader to focus on Programmes that are worth keeping; Programmes should be assessed based on whether there will be increased Academic Performance for all Students. Meeting frequently with the Budget Team can improve Problem-solving and increase Motivation, while preparing them for errors and disruptions. Delegating Work to Others is an important task in the Budget Process. According to the author, the School Leader should practice Reflective Techniques so as not to lose sight of Critical Tactics.

Making Optimal Use of Available Resources

There is a need for Leaders in Education to be effective Financial Managers and comply with Financial Policies and Procedures and also, according to the author, hone Selection Skills when involved in Tactical Decisions. School Leaders will benefit from an effective Instructional Programme and therefore, it is important to check the Plan for completeness when strategically aligning Resources with Pedagogical Purpose. Careful alignment of Resources in support of the School Improvement Plan will promote Student Success.

While Student Success is the ultimate goal for all Schools, the focus has to be on Specific Goals and Strategies for Improvement in order to make a lasting difference. The School Improvement Plan outlines changes a School needs to make to improve the Student Achievement Level and demonstrate the ways that these changes will be made. The School Improvement Plan involves all Staff Members in Planning, Implementing, Monitoring, and Refining; the Plan is drawn from a variety of sources, such as, Instructional Data and Student Achievement Data.

Importantly, the School Improvement Plan informs the School Budget and, therefore, the Budget Process needs to be transparent and should reflect School Priorities. The best School Improvement Plan includes activities that cover a significant portion of the overall Annual School Budget. Today, School Leaders need to invest their Time and Resources in Programmes with Confidence. Careful Monitoring and Targeted Support will reduce wastage of Resources. It is vital that School Leaders develop creative solutions for addressing Student Needs. A range of Programmes should be implemented so as to make the most effective use of Available Resources to enhance Teaching and Learning. The School should ensure that the Human and Physical Resources address the needs of the Students.

There are continued echoes from Professional and the Political arenas regarding the need for Effective School Leaders. School Administrators should not leave the responsibility and knowledge of their Budgets to others. Principals are failing due to Mismanagement of Student Accounts than any other reason and, therefore, it is vital to have their Executive Assistants check the Line Items on the Budget to prevent shortages in any area. Legitimately, it is appropriate for the School to spend what has been budgeted. It is not advisable to have large surpluses towards the end of the fiscal year, as this is considered a sign that the School did not need these funds.

According to English (2011), School Budgets are an integral part of Plans, Processes, and Productivity. School Leaders should explicate ways and means of planning and managing fiscal operations. Budgeting is a form of planning and School Leaders are vested with the responsibility to plan Resources, Procurements, and Disbursements within the context of School Improvement and Student Achievement. Leaders in Education are faced with challenges of increasing costs, diminishing resources, and rising expectations.

The authors suggested that Schools are expected to be transparent by obtaining and providing reliable, relevant, and consistent information to Staff Members and Stakeholders, on their financial situation and characteristics. School Administrators should seek to provide the Community with ongoing understanding of information contained in financial records. It was further argued that School Leaders support Public Officials and provide guidance when implementing Financial Plans. The School Goals should be clearly stated and Reported Performance Information should be aligned with the missions, goals, and objectives, as set forth in a Strategic Plan, Budget, or other sources. Also, included in this Plan, should be information relating to Resources utilized or Costs of Programmes or Services. When faced with inconsistent patterns of Expenditure in Schools, Teachers and School Leaders may view the Resource Allocation Process as unfair and suspicious. It is fundamental that School Finance Plans and Reports provide detailed Expenditures by Programme or Activity.

FINANCIAL PLANNING

Planning is the foundation of Goals and Objectives, it describes various methods and responsibilities required to achieve those Goals, and establish a timeline for accomplishing the Goals and Objectives. Engaging in the Budget Process confirms commitment to the organization and can serve as means of control and change. Proper Fiscal Operations Control and Sound Planning are essential in achieving Public Confidence.

English (2011) suggested that Public Confidence in a Community is based on Economic Practices and requires performance of the following tasks:
- Prudence: Promoting Efficiency and keeping the "house" in order
- Alignment: Balancing Revenues and Expenditures
- Performance: Demonstrating Results aligned with School Goals

Let us examine the importance of Setting Priorities.

For the School Leader, Setting Priorities is an essential task. School Leaders are often involved in short- or long-range Planning, such as:
- Purchasing Musical Instruments versus Maintaining the Library Hours of 5 days per week

Communities need to rely on results if they are to continue supporting their Schools. To ensure that the Budget is easily understood by the Public, it is vital for School Administrators to translate educational priorities into financial terms. Planning is fundamental to School Leadership, since Fiscal Operations do impact Achievement Scores and Range of Course Offerings.

Graham-Blake (2002) stated that a School Budget is a Statement of Estimated Expenditure and Financial Proposals that is presented to the Ministry of Education for the ensuing year. Once approved, the Statement is official. The Principal prepares the important document in consultation with School Administrators including Vice Principals, Department Heads, and Senior Teachers. The first step in the Budget Process is to analyze the Budget from the previous year in order to ascertain the shortfall and to determine how well the needs of that year were met. It was further stated that a designated person, usually the Chairman, ensures that all Expenditures in the form of cheques are receipted, and follow the proper procedures.

The Budget outlines how the Resources should be allocated and according to Graham-Blake (2002), the Principal has to operate within the Approved Budget. The Resources itemized in the Budget are used to make the following payments:
- Academic Staff
- Administrative Staff
- Ancillary Staff
- Instructional Materials
- Maintenance and Repairs
- Vehicle Upkeep
- Utilities
- Canteen
- Instructional Materials
- Sanitation

Fundamental to the Budget, are notes of short descriptions of intended Purchases and Costs. School Resources can be received in the following ways:
- Cash
- Materials
- Labour
- Equipment
- Gifts from Organizations (Ministry of Education, Private Voluntary Organizations, Social Investment Funds, Churches, Private Enterprises, Members of Parliament,

Parent Teachers' Associations, Clubs, Past Students' Associations), Institutions, and Individuals.

According to Sohan (2002), the School Budget is a summary of Proposed Programmes in the School that will be reflected by the Anticipated Revenues. It is vital that School Leaders ensure that the Budget is properly prepared and administered. The Budget allows for Achievement of the Objectives of the School; Expenditure Planning; System of Control; and Best Measures to be Implemented for Responsible Persons to Improve Performance. The Bursar has an important role of accountability for all spending, continuously monitoring, reporting on operations of the Budget, and presenting updated accounting records to Auditors, when necessary. The Report should be submitted to the Ministry of Education and the Chairman.

DEVELOPING DEPARTMENT BUDGETS

The Department Head should ensure that the Goals and Objectives of the Department support and further the Goals and Objectives of the School. One of the key Budgetary Planning Processes is preparing the Department Budget. The Department Budget is a collaborative process of the Fiscal Operations reflecting the Goals of the Department. Department Requisitions are made each year which include the following:
- Priorities
- Ongoing Expenditures, including Replacement of Chairs, Desks, Chalk Boards
- Instructional Materials, including Classroom Materials, Field Trips, Professional Development

- Capital Outlay, including Adding a Staff Lounge, Classroom, Bathroom

Let us consider the factors involved in developing the Department Budget, some of which are listed below:
- The Budget from the Previous Year
- Actual Enrollment in the various Programme Areas
- Adjustment to Programme Offerings
- Teacher Replacements
- New Teaching and Non-Teaching Positions
- Adjustments to Operating Costs, such as, Supplies

A good starting point for the Department Budgeting Process is collaborating with Team Members in the Department. The Team will gather Past, Actual, and Current Year-to-Date Records. The next step is to define and evaluate Department Goals by asking questions, such as:
- What are the Expectations of the Department?
- What is Management looking for?

Prioritize these Goals and discuss which course of action will work best. Coordinating with other Departments is always a helpful source. During this Process, it is always a good idea to present various scenarios to show experience.

Regular Review of the Progress ensures that Goals are being met and the Team is operating within the Budget. Adjustments can be made, as necessary.

Once consensus is established on revised Tactics, and Costs and Revenues are assigned, the Budget is derived. Department Heads are responsible for implementing the documented Strategies.

Details about each Activity need to be outlined, such as, Individuals responsible for the Action, how the Plan will be Monitored, and Estimated Costs and Revenues for Executing the Tactic.

When Schools are supported by strong Leadership Teams that are transparent and challenge the Spending, they can make significant efficient gains. Efficient Departments maximize their spending in Activities and Learning Resources that make the greatest difference to Student Outcomes, and need to be creative in minimizing all other operating costs. Schools should continuously seek ways to optimize their Spending Decisions to achieve the best Outcomes for their Students. When Departments are involved in the Budget Building Process, they have the opportunity to make their Sourcing Decisions that best suits their own context and circumstances.

LEADERSHIP REFLECTION

When in the School Year, is information requested for Budgets from Departments or Committees?
_____
_____
_____

Create FIVE Ethical Guidelines for Staff Members who are new Participants in the School Budgetary Process
_____
_____
_____
_____
_____
_____

Does the Department Budget Timing serve the School well, or would you like to see it Timed differently?

BUDGETING AS A TOOL TO DRIVE CURRICULUM DELIVERY AND STUDENT SUCCESS

The School Leader plays an important role in sharing their knowledge and expertise in Facilitating, Communicating, and Managing Results that contribute to Academic Success of its Students, and Instructional and Whole-School Performance. It is vital that the School have the right Resources to support the changing needs of the Curriculum. The Budget should be aligned to High-quality Teaching and Student Success. Hence, Budget Development is a cross-departmental activity which is dependent on all individuals actively participating, holding themselves accountable for complying with policies, and meeting deadlines associated with their individual roles.

An effective School Leader will channel the Resources to areas of need or development, which will result in the School achieving its

Goals and Objectives.

CURRICULUM REFORM CHECKLIST

CURRICULUM DEVELOPMENT	YES	NO	COMMENTS
Introduce changes to Curriculum based on Research			
Strengthen the range of Vocational Subjects to address labour market needs			
Offer a more varied and relevant Curriculum that has opportunities to study Practical Subjects, such as, Drama, Art, Music			
Provide alternative Programmes for Non-Academic Students			
Promote Multi-literate (critical thinkers, ICT literate, problem-solvers)			
Offer ICT as a Core Subject			
Offer a broader Formal and Informal Curriculum			
A more appropriate Curriculum for all Learners			
Provide Cross-curricular Learning			
Promote opportunities for Sports and qualifications in Sports			
Offer more non-School related Educational Sessions, Debates, Competitions, Public Speaking			
Offer more Extra-curricular Activities			

| Provide Outdoor Activities related directly to engage Teachers and Students | | | |

LEADERSHIP REFLECTION

Examine ONE Budget from a Secondary School and ONE Budget from a Primary School
Compare both Budgets

_____
_____
_____
_____
_____
_____
_____
_____
_____
_____
_____
_____
_____
_____
_____
_____
_____
_____
_____
_____
_____
_____
_____
_____

Examine TWO Budgets from Schools at the same Educational Level
Compare Both Budgets

_____
_____
_____
_____
_____
_____
_____
_____
_____
_____
_____
_____
_____
_____
_____
_____
_____
_____
_____
_____
_____
_____
_____
_____
_____
_____
_____

A name brand Athletic Shoe Company has approached your School with a Proposal to have their Logo and Advertising Signs installed on your School Buses which cost a considerable amount.

Explain TWO implications that this type of Decision may have on your School

___

Discuss THREE Ways that the Curriculum Department Budget Process can empower and engender Accountability of Subject Leaders

___

_____
_____
_____
_____
_____
_____
_____
_____

Develop a Priority Rating Score Criteria that will show which IT Programmes should be undertaken first

Priority 1

_____
_____
_____

Priority 2

_____
_____
_____

Priority 3

_____
_____
_____

Seifert (2002) stated that a School Administrator is a Leader in Education who promotes Student Success by ensuring Management of the Organization, Operations, and Resources for a safe, efficient, and effective learning environment. Budgeting is planning for every

activity that is taking place in a School. Budget Decisions may include the following:
- Additional Staff Members
- Adjustments to Personnel Assignments
- Additional Supplies and Materials

Budgeting should be part of new Decisions and Programme Changes which can take a period of six months or longer, such as, Curriculum Design and Instructional Modifications. School Leaders make recommendations as to what Resources are required to offer the Programmes that will achieve the Goals for their educational context. Schools use a range of Stakeholders to drive the Budget Decisions to request funds.

A Budget Calendar is used by the Budget Team, according to Seifert (2002), to develop the Budget in a time-sensitive manner and should include:
- List of Activities
- Time needed for each Activity
- Dates for Initiation and completion of tasks

Planning and preliminary steps are developed by the Budget Team, to organize the development process, such as, Student Projections; School and Department Expenditure Requests, Revenue Estimates, and Preparation of the Budget Document.

Let us consider the following Strategies that School Leaders may employ:
- Delaying Recruitment of some posts in line with Student Enrolment
- Increasing Teaching Commitments of some of the Senior Leadership Team

- Varying Distribution of Responsibilities across Staff Levels

Some of these Strategies may not appear attractive in the first instance; however, reality dictates that necessary adjustments may have to be made. At times, these Adjustments are relevant in the Budget Building Process. The Budget needs to demonstrate the viability of the Strategic Plan. Decisions should be explained in a written narrative accompanying the Strategic Plan.

BUDGET REVIEW STRATEGY

Budget Reviews ensure the financial security of the School from month-to-month and year-to-year. Effective School Leaders maintain financial control of the Budget by reviewing the current position and taking the necessary action. Regular monitoring of Income and Expenditure against the Budget is essential for Schools for the reasons enumerated below:
- Additional Funding may become available during the School Year resulting in larger Surplus than expected
- Unexpected Expenditures may be presented, such as, additional Staff Members
- Budgeted Private Funding may not materialize for various reasons
- The expected number of Enrolled Students may differ from the Budget approved figures
- Other Assumptions can be inaccurate at the time the Budget was prepared

It is of utmost importance that the School Administrator has a thorough understanding of the School Finance. Simply relying on others can lead to inaccurate decisions. The School Leader should be in a position, at all times, to provide clear and detailed explanations of financial best practices to Staff Members and Stakeholders, by networking with other Administrators and Financial Experts; seeking support from the Financial Advisors in the Ministry of Education in their Region; and being Proactive.

Let us examine the Responsibilities of a Newly Appointed School Leader, as it relates to the understanding of the Budget.

At the start of the assignment, the newly appointed School Leader should gather the available Financial Reports from the previous Accounting Year, in order to build a picture of the Resourcing Position of the School. Checking the Financial Position of the School will ensure that the appropriate Resourcing Decisions are made. It is vital, also, to research information on the Student Enrollment, Staff Members, and the Community.

The core purpose of Strategic Planning and Budgeting in Schools is to focus on improving Student Outcomes, thus maximizing the potential for all Students. There is external pressure on Schools to improve Financial Efficiency. Sometimes the link between what is spent, how it is spent, and the Student Achievement Outcomes is complex, and the drive to improve Outcomes does not always result in greater efficiency in Schools. Highly-skilled Financial Managers have the ability to scrutinize Expenditure and achieve value for money. Today, with more Accountability and Reporting roles, School Leaders are challenged to focus more attention on Efficiency.

LEADERSHIP REFLECTION

If you had to make ONE Change to your Budget Process, what would it be?

_____
_____
_____
_____
_____
_____

State the Reason(s) for your Recommendations

_____
_____
_____
_____
_____

Outline TWO Priority Areas that Resources are targeted in your Educational Context

_____
_____
_____
_____
_____

Describe TWO Ways in which your School ensures that its Budget is developed to support its Strategic Plan and other Stated Priorities

_____
_____

Develop a Curriculum Instructional Improvement Plan for your School, to be presented to the Board of Management for Approval. Include a Budget

How effectively do Current Budget-Setting Practices in your Educational Context, ensure that Spending Decisions minimize Costs and maximize Student Outcomes?

_____
_____
_____
_____
_____
_____
_____
_____
_____
_____

To what extent, do you think the following Specialist Skills and Knowledge are necessary for the Decision-makers in your Educational Context?

Financial Expertise

_____
_____
_____
_____
_____

Strategic and in-depth understanding of School Operations and other key issues

_____
_____

Common sense, and having the right attitude and experience

Commercial and Procurement Skills

How does (Does) your School utilize any of the following Strategic Approaches that are particularly innovative and effective?
Networking Skills

Pooling of Resources

Collaborative Procurement

5
CURRICULUM, INSTRUCTION, AND STUDENT SUCCESS FROM AN INTERNATIONAL PERSPECTIVE

Curriculum design requires insight of the needs of Students and their anticipated outcomes. It has to be Student-focused and engaging. The Curriculum should reflect the local community needs, while recognizing the global demands.

The implementation of the Curriculum that is all encompassing requires Teachers, Managers and Administrators with the Vision and Professional Capacity to direct the Students to success. The Leadership Skills required to promote the implementation is critical, because the magnitude of the task of bringing all the Stakeholders together is significant. The Stakeholders will have to be engaged in the process of focusing on the big picture, which is Student Success. When the Stakeholders are effectively engaged in the stages of Design and Implementation of the Curriculum, a successful outcome is more predictable. The involvement of Stakeholders that represent the various levels of communities will show that the School Leadership is thinking about the Local, National, and Global impact of such Design and Implementation.
When an innovative Curriculum has been Designed and Implemented, it needs to be assessed based on the Standard established by the governing bodies in the Discipline. A strong effective Leadership and Professional staff working with the students will heighten student engagement and enhance the possibility of meeting and surpassing the Assessment expectations.

In order to promote Student Success, the Leadership will need to create an environment that fosters Professional Development and opens Communication for staff.

A Professional is an individual with specialized skill, knowledge, and a repertoire of behaviours needed in their Practice. A Professional must operate according to a standard of Principles and Theories utilized by Members of the Profession when making decisions. Strong, consistent, integrated internal practices constitute Professionalism.

Let us examine the fundamental, identifying characteristics of the Teaching Profession.

Competence and Professionalism should be demonstrated to Colleagues through regular interactions, and conducted with honesty and integrity. It is the responsibility of the School Leader to study how to better understand and serve the needs of their Students. Most importantly, Students are of utmost priority, and assigning blame to others completely undermines the ability to work professionally. Training and experience informs the Professional on how to prepare.

Professionalism is the cornerstone of Teaching Practice. School Leaders should demonstrate their commitment to Students, Learning, and the Profession of Teaching. Leadership within the Education System is supporting the Vision when they promote a high degree of Professionalism. In support of Professionalism, School Leaders actively empower Teachers to make positive changes in the Learning Environment and Schools including, accessing Tools and Technologies used in their Profession. Also, the Leader in Education ensures adherence to School and Ministry Procedures.

SELF-REFLECTION

Self-Reflection is a core attribute of human activity. It is vital that individuals engage in Reflective Thinking by examining the wholeness of their thoughts, actions, and motivation levels. Effective School Leaders make the necessary adjustments with the support of Mentors and Coaches.

Let us examine the various opportunities available to a School Professional when they engage in Reflective Practice.
- Collegial Conversations
- Journal Writing
- Examining the Work of Students
- Informal Observations and Conversations
- Thoughts relating to Teaching
- Focus on Lesson Revisions and Effective Instruction
- Mentors, Coaches, and Supervisors

What are the Benefits of Honest and Frequent Reflections?
_____
_____
_____
_____
_____
_____
_____

Describe TWO Ways in which you evaluate your Instructional

Effectiveness?

Describe TWO Benefits that you have gained from Collaborative Experiences in your Educational Context

TRUST BUILDING USING PARALANGUAGE, RESPONSE BEHAVIOUR, AND DIAGNOSTIC TOOLS

Trust is an extremely vital commodity to the School Leader and can build professional and personal relationships. Trust is strengthened when an individual interacts with others. It is important to pay attention to Paralanguage or Sounds when used as a method of communication, in verbal exchanges. Listening carefully is an essential skill for Effective Communication. Active Listening develops Trust when engaging in Partnerships or Productive Relationships. Paralanguage involves Speech, Rate, Volume, and Pitch, and helps the School Leader to build rapport. Once rapport is established, Trust is enhanced, Barriers are reduced, and Exchange of Information is improved.

The School Leader needs to be aware of the Rapport Indicators. Let us consider the various ways that individuals express themselves.
- Voice – Fast or Slow
- Tone – Soft or Loud
- Tempo – High or Low

Employing a technique that matches each individual, helps build Trust and it will demonstrate the genuine interest in communication and understanding.

Leaders in Education need to be more candid and authentic in Trust Building. Being accessible and not delegating the task of Communication is an important way to get started in the Trust Building process. The Leader who takes time to listen to Staff concerns is creating opportunities for dialogue in promoting the Vision of reducing the gap in Student Achievement. Dependability and reliability are characteristics of a Good Leader. Tasks completed within the time promised, speak volumes for the Administrator.

Diagnostic Tools are response to a series of Questions or

Statements in any field, either in writing or verbally, and indicates an ability or interest in a particular field. Diagnostic Tools are valid, reliable Self-reporting Trust Scales. When these Diagnostic Tools are employed, they provide insights to help the Leaders and Followers understand their Trust Dynamics in their relationships, improve performance, and attain their Goals.

MEDIATIONAL DISCOURSE REFLECTION

Reflection is an effective tool in Teaching Practice and involves critique. Some Learning takes place alone and some involve other individuals. Learning is a Participatory activity. There is significantly greater meaning when an activity is done with Reflection. This adds value to the fact that an active exercise is required to enhance the Teaching and Learning process. When Reflection takes place, it is a search for greater understanding and inspiration. Reflection fosters growth and may be categorized as an Ethical Responsibility for Educators.

Every Student is unique, with different personalities, and different learning patterns. It is the responsibility of the Teacher to reflect on the Learning Process and Practice to advance in their Profession. Only through Reflective Practice will Teachers understand the nature of their Practice, Potential, and Pedagogy. It is while Reflecting on work, new interpretations of the meaning are born. The School Administrator that engages in Reflective Practices will remain open to continuous Learning.

COMMITMENT TO STUDENT LEARNING

It is important for Teachers to utilize Teaching Methods that enable small steps towards achieving their overall Goals. The Teacher should focus on completing the task which will enhance the achievement of the Goals. When the task is meaningful to the Student, there tends to be true commitment to the task.

There will be common joy in the Learning Environment when the Teacher demonstrates genuine interest and provide opportunities for Students to participate in their own learning. Teachers can provide opportunities for experiencing the joy of learning by thinking of a range of Teaching Methods to enhance Student Learning. It is important for Students to be motivated to pursue Excellence by teaching Work Ethics that supports the following;
- The desire for them to perform at their best
- Determination to overcome challenges,
- Attention to small details,
- An awareness of how initiative, integrity, responsibility, diligence,
- and determination influence the actions and behaviours of Students in the Classroom.

PERFORMANCE AND TEACHER ASSESSMENT PROGRESS REPORTS

The Cross Sectoral Assessment Working Party (2011) stated that Assessment is the process of obtaining and carefully interpreting the evidence to make decisions about Student Learning. There is a major bond between Learning Outcomes, Content, and Teaching and Learning Activities. The Aim of Assessment is to improve Learning, Inform Teaching, support Students in achieving the highest standards they can, and provide purposeful Reports on Student Achievement.

Assessments play multiple roles in Education and send signals regarding Student Achievement and take the form of Classroom Tests, Formative Classroom Assessments, and Local/National Tests. Assessment yield tangible results and it is a vehicle to inform School, Teachers, Students, and Policy Makers about Student Achievement. It is important that Teachers continuously assess what their Students know and focus on how they derive at their understanding by reviewing homework, listening to student conversations, asking questions, responding to questions, and observing Learning Strategies. Regular Summative Assessments will build Student understanding. Teachers compile their Assessment from Assessment Materials, Textbooks, Workbooks, Personal Classroom Experiences, Experiences with Standardized Assessments (Multiple Choice Tests, Writing Assignments, Projects, Portfolios guided by Rubrics), Collaborations with Colleagues, and Professional Development Initiatives. Teachers continually assess Student Progress, analyze the results, and adjust Instruction to improve Student Performance.

Assessments can be very supportive tools and can signal Educators to adjust their Practices, and for Leaders to modify their Policies in an effort to make informed decisions. Individual Teachers, Students, and Schools can assess their own progress in terms of educational accomplishments. Policy Makers and Educators can ensure there is alignment in Content, Instruction, and Assessment at all levels of the Education System. Assessments help shape instruction and increase the level of expectation for Student Performance. In addition, Assessments support accountability.

Formative Assessment for Learning is used by Teachers at the start and during the Instructional Process. Students reflect on and monitor their own progress; the information informs Teachers on decisions regarding Quality of Teaching and Learning. Summative Assessment of Learning, on the other hand, is used at the end of the Instruction Period. This type of Assessment provides information on the Effectiveness of Teaching Strategies, the Time required for Instruction and Recommendations for Improvements for future Student Learning (The Cross Sectoral Assessment Working Party, 2011).

Let us examine situations where Teachers restrict their expectations for Student Learning to particular knowledge and skills to be addressed in the Test. Should School Administrators play police officers to ensure that Teachers are not involved in inappropriate Test Preparation Practices, such as, Item-Teaching.

- Are Teachers pressured to raise their Test Scores?
- Are Teachers focusing on School Performance compared to National Test Performance?

LEADERSHIP REFLECTION

June Smith, Grade 5 Teacher, consulted the Narrative accompanying National Standardized Achievement Tests and found that the Descriptions stated were inadequate and ambiguous to guide her Instructions for her Grade 5 Students. June simply aimed her Instruction at the knowledge and skills represented by the Test Items. Frustrated by the intense pressure to improve her Student Scores, June engaged in some full-scale Item-Teaching. One of her friends had copies of the Test that her Students will take and lends it to June for a few days so that June can understand the Content that has to be mastered by her Students. June had a few Test-targeted Sessions with her Students and used actual items taken from the Test. Most Students scored very well. Her Students last year scored on average in the 40th percentile, but this year, her Students earned a Mean Score equal to the 86th percentile.

June is reluctant to reveal to Colleagues and Administration that she relied on Item-teaching Practice.

How could you determine, as the School Administrator, that the Grade 5 Test Scores for this year were based on the Item-coaching and not Good Instruction?

___

State the Difference between Item-teaching and Curriculum-teaching and discuss the impact each may have on the learning process.

___

Outline the Benefits to be derived from challenging Students to move beyond the limits of their current knowledge or understanding

SUPERVISION OF INSTRUCTION

Student Learning is one of the most critical responsibilities of the Administrator. It is important that Administrators reinforce and enhance Teaching Practices through the Effective Supervision of Instruction. This Administrative Task leads to Student Learning Improvement. Feedback and direction to Teachers are crucial for the Supervision process to be meaningful. Careful analysis of Teacher Performance and appropriate Data will assist Administrators when providing Feedback to Teachers (Fischer, n.d.). Teachers are held accountable for providing an appropriate, well-planned programme, which includes introduction of a variety of Teaching Strategies designed to address the Diverse Needs of all Students in a changing society.

Fischer (n.d.) suggested that it is the role of the Administrator to enhance the Professional Effectiveness of the Teachers. The Administrator should ensure that they possess a repertoire of skills to guide Teachers in improving Instruction, such as, What to Evaluate; How to Observe and Analyze Classroom Information and other data; and How to transfer the Results of Observation and Summary of Data into meaningful Feedback. These skills will support the Administrator when assessing whether Teachers are utilizing the various Formative and Summative Assessments available for successful and meaningful planning.

Supervisors are required to have in-depth knowledge and understanding of Instructional Theory and according to Fischer (n.d), they should be based on the following Checklist:
- Gathering Data
- Teacher Conferencing
- Planning the Conference
- Memorandum and Letters of Reprimand

There are three main sources of information to determine the competency level of Teachers – Observations, Interviews, and Documents. Weekly 'Walk-throughs' lasting for brief periods, are conducted in order to identify ongoing patterns of behaviour. The 'Walk-through' is normally unannounced and a Written Summary or Conference with the Teacher would follow these Informal Observations. Formal Observations, on the other hand, is announced and usually takes the form of an agreed-upon time. The Pre- and Post-Conferences and Written Summary all form part of the Formal Observation Process. A Description of the Conference, Observation, Judgments of the Observer, Agreements for changes in Teacher Behaviours, Activities, Classroom Environments are contained in the Summary. Interviews can include Discussions with Students, Parents, and Administrative Team Members, in which they provide their views. Various types of documents can provide the relevant information, such as, Student Letters, Complaint Forms, Information submitted by Students, Folders, and Portfolios.

Administrators should engage themselves in Conferences throughout the year in an effort to support the Teacher in making improvements to Concepts, Knowledge, and increasing understanding of the School Goals. The Pre-Conference is held prior to the Formal Observation and is a source of information about the upcoming Observation. Post Conferences are planned by the Administrator in order to achieve a particular Goal. Teachers, in a Collaborative Approach with the Administrator, can identify problem areas, develop data, and share the willingness to grow professionally.

To start the process, it is designed that Teachers present an overview and their analysis of the Lesson that was observed. The Administrator directs and monitors the Follow-up Activities, following the Conference. The purpose of the Written Statement, at the end of the process, is to clearly outline the expected changes, and recommendations for the Professional Development Activities, where appropriate. The Monitoring Process provides information on whether the desired changes have taken place and should be documented. The Administrator reviews the Data identifying strengths and areas of concern prior to the Conference.

Prior to the Conference, it is vital to think of questions that will help Teachers to focus on the areas of concern or matters to clarify. Well-organized thoughts will ensure that the session is kept in a timely manner. Enhancement and Improvement are the key elements of the Conference.

Following the Conference, the Teacher should receive a Summary in Writing, on his performance or conduct. Specific facts should be documented, including date, time, place, other personnel that were present, performance or action of Students, Teachers, Administrators, and Unit or Lesson should be described. Oral and written Compliments and Complaints should be noted. The Teacher should be given the right to respond.

LEADERSHIP REFLECTION

Interview TWO Teachers to ascertain the most Effective Processes and Behaviours demonstrated by their Supervisors, when supporting them in improving their Teaching.

Provide a Summary of the Interview

_____
_____
_____
_____
_____
_____
_____
_____
_____
_____
_____

Describe the Differences and Similarities in the TWO Perspectives presented.

Provide your Reaction to the Findings

Describe TWO important Skills that an Administrator must possess to improve the Quality and Diversity of Instruction in the School

Discuss TWO Strategies that a School Leader can utilize to support the Teacher in improving Instructional Opportunities for Students

QUALITY FEEDBACK

Feeney (2007) suggested that the aim of Feedback is to improve effectiveness of Teaching and promote Professional Growth. It is important for School Administrators to focus attention on the Annual Evaluation Process and the positive impact it has on Teacher Growth and Student Learning. Through collective efforts, Administrators and Teachers should utilize their reservoir of skills to establish Professional Goals that focus on Student Learning Outcomes. Quality Instruction provided by Teachers is of utmost importance to Student Achievement.

Feedback is an essential Assessment Tool. Quality Feedback is a thoughtful process because it informs Teaching and creates meaningful Goals for Professional Growth of the Teacher. The Effective Leader in Education ensures that Feedback includes meaningful comments and should be cognizant that Feedback without links to Student Learning can result in diminished capacity over time (Feeney, 2007). The School Leader should provide opportunities for Teachers to engage in Data Analysis and connect Instruction and Student Learning. Constructive Feedback can promote Reflection, thereby focusing on new Goals. Improvement will take place if the individual is self-motivated, which will not be likely from External Feedback alone.

Let us consider Teacher Feedback that includes Reflective Inquiry: "A Recommendation for Ms. Gordon to continue to reflect her commitment to Differentiated Instruction to meet the diverse needs of Students." In supporting these Students Ms. Gordon can incorporate the suggested Reading Strategies during each Phase of Comprehension and Vocabulary Development."
- Pre-Reading: KWL, Brainstorming
- During Reading: Paired Reading, Graphic Organizers
- Reflection Strategy: Group Summary, Class Discussions

Teachers should be encouraged to search for new Tools and Strategies.

Let us examine the following Student-centred Approach.
During a Lesson, the Teacher asks the Students the following questions:
- What are you learning?
- Why do you think it is important to learn this Topic?

In establishing Professional Goals, Teachers will reconsider their approach to Planning, Instruction, and Assessment if they spend the time looking at Learning from the Student Perspective.

A Performance Rubric is a useful guide for Administrators and outlines the effective Features of Teaching that can be utilized throughout the Evaluation Process. Evaluators provide direction to Teachers through its use. A Collaborative Approach between Administrators and Teachers throughout the School Year will provide opportunities for Clarifying, Problem-solving, Negotiating, and Presenting. According to Feeney (2007), the Performance Rubric acts as common language when providing Summative Evaluation.

NETWORKING AND LEARNING COMMUNITIES

School Leaders are sometimes trained in the technical aspects of work. Let us examine the typical tasks of a traditional School Leader.
- Developing Schedules
- Preparing Budgets
- Hosting Parent Meetings

Today, Peers can support each other in Networked Learning. When like-minds collaborate, there is an opportunity for Administrators to coach each other by utilizing their problem-solving skills and becoming 21st Century Leaders in Education and reduce the gaps in Student Achievement.

School Leaders engage with other colleagues from different Schools and share best practices, challenges, and issues that promote or inhibit their individual Leadership efforts. Conditions are created for Administrators to study their collective practices. The foundations of rich Network Learning Cultures are based on Trust, Inquiry-based Practice, and Shared Leadership. School Leaders foster relationships among diverse groups when they share, listen, learn, take steps to increase Leadership Capacity, and attain high levels of Student Achievement.

It is fundamental for School Administrators to be open to outside Learning Sources, so that they can apply what is learned from colleagues, in their Schools. A Network of Colleagues provides a form of assurance, encouragement, and inspiration for the School Administrator, as they visit other Schools, share Resources, and develop collective ownership.

PEER REVIEW TEACHER ASSESSMENT

Teachers have the expertise and skills to provide Feedback on their Fellow Teachers. The Peer Reviews are utilized when evaluating whether Fellow Teachers meet performance standards. For the Peer Review Process to be effective, Teachers should not only evaluate their Peers, but provide support.

An increasing number of Instructors are undertaking Peer Review where colleagues are invited to visit classes and provide Feedback. However, the first time visit can be an unsettling experience for even the experienced Teacher (Farrell, 2011). Some Teachers go as far as perceiving the Peer Review as a Plan to set colleagues up against each other.

Effective School Administrators elevate the Professional Culture of the School and support for Teachers as they improve their teaching. The Peer Review Process is supported by the Administrator by building Trust among colleagues, while maintaining high expectations. Detailed Rubrics for each standard can assist Fellow Teachers to identify Best Practices in the Classroom, when conducting Peer Review.

The School Leader should support Peer Review Initiatives and participate by setting clear guidelines for conducting the Peer Review; also, providing supporting Materials and Resources. Peer Review differs from the traditional Evaluation Methods, and according to Farrell (2011), it allows an individual to receive Feedback on their Teaching. Fellow Teachers are in a unique position to provide insights and suggestions, because they understand the complexities of Teaching, and also, based on the classroom experiences they can share.

Firstly, let us reflect on an entire Department adopting Peer Review as a Collaborative Approach that has great potential to improve learning. It is important that the Peer Review is used to support colleagues in Diverse Approaches to Teaching; Critical Reflection on their Teaching; and informing the Evaluation Process of Strategies to Support Teachers in any area of improvement.

Secondly, let us take a further look at a Reciprocal Departmental Peer Review where colleagues take turns observing as a Reviewee and Reviewer for the other. It is not a requirement for both Reviewer and Reviewee to have the same number of years of experience nor the same qualification, or classification. Teachers in the Department will share responsibility for Quality Teaching.

In the Reciprocal Review, Teachers are more likely to approach their role with Respect and Collegiality, when it is a two-way process, rather than a one-way process as described in the first Reflection. The Reciprocal Peer Review Evaluation will represent a body of achievement over time.

LEADERSHIP REFLECTION

Create a Peer Review Rubric that can be used in your Educational Context to improve Teacher Evaluation

_____
_____
_____
_____
_____
_____
_____

LEARNING NEEDS OF STUDENTS

It is vital that School Administrators utilize research on critical issues, such as, Student Motivation, Learning, and Retention; Special Needs; and embrace generally accepted Global Practices. The Leadership Team should be committed and Student-centred, making decisions on School Policies, Curriculum, and related School Programmes. Students should be treated as individuals and their strengths recognized. The School Leader should focus on identifying the educational needs of Students and take proactive steps to maximize support for meeting those needs. "Individualism" is promoted when Administrators respect the contributions of all Students and support Differentiated Instruction in a continuous effort to attain the potential of the Student.

Leithwood, et al (2004) stated that School Leaders should

recognize the importance of the Pedagogical Content Knowledge of Teachers in relation to School Effectiveness; in addition, the Professional Community that is built by colleagues inside and outside their educational context. Student Learning varies according to Class Size, Student-grouping Practices, Instructional Practices, and the inherent features and scope of Monitoring Student Progress. It is essential for School Administrators to employ Decision-making Techniques to adopt the features that achieve positive influence on the Learning Needs of Students, depending on their educational context. Research provides an appreciation of Educational Practices to improve overall quality and significantly add value to Student Outcomes.

Lewis, et al (2015) suggested that Information on what Students know, what they should know, and Strategies required to meet those Academic Needs can be extracted from Data Analysis. Educators are informed by multiple data sources.

Let us examine the information that School Leaders collect from this enormous Data.
- Student Attendance
- Behaviour
- Performance
- Administrative and Perpetual Data

School Leaders should not only focus on the Quantity but the Quality of Information, which informs them about how the information is used. The Data can assist Teachers in analyzing Assessment Results and Student Work Samples; Student Work is extremely informative when deciding Learning Instructional Needs. Teachers can collaborate regularly to analyze, interpret, and use

Data to adjust Instruction and plan lessons. Data will identify where Students need improvement in understanding a concept.

Let us examine the ways that Capacity Building can improve Instruction with Teacher Collaborative Approaches.
- Training in analyzing Student Work
- Use of Common Assessments to determine Student Success
- Teachers plan and implement Standard-based Lessons
- Refine Instruction to include Strategies, such as, Scaffolding to meet Enrichment Needs
- Team Discussions focus on how to improve future Instruction.

Let us now consider how School Leadership Teams can meet the needs of Students.

The Effective Leadership Team will engage in a process of Review of the Quality of the Learning Environment for the School as a whole and within individual classrooms. The aim of this process is to ensure a School Environment that provides well-structured and culturally-engaging Teaching and Learning Activities, with a focus on active participation.

CHECKLIST FOR IDENTIFYING LEARNING NEEDS OF STUDENTS

	YES	NO	COMMENTS
Do you accommodate Instruction that best reflects the Learning Styles of the Students?			

Do you encourage purposeful dialogue in the classroom?			
Are the prior background experiences of Students taken into account when current skills are being taught?			
Do you value and incorporate the use of Diverse Community Practices in the Curriculum?			
Are Students strategically in ongoing Instructional dialogue to support expression of ideas?			
Do you provide opportunities for Students to utilize Higher-order Thinking and Scaffolding?			

Administrators should engage in discussions with Teachers on the benefits of participating in Professional Development Initiatives that will support them in developing strategies to meet the Learning Needs of all Students. Fundamental to the overall Student Achievement is the Leader in Education, who provides Effective Practices to support Students and utilizes Progress Monitoring Data to inform interventions.

Let us examine a Leadership Team that is committed to the Learning Needs of Students. These Leaders will utilize their collective skills and experience to:

- Support and empower Parents and Students toward Academic Success
- Support Teachers by providing Professional Development opportunities, Instructional Materials, and engaging and appropriate Instruction
- Incorporate a variety of Student Assessments to measure Student Progress, such as, Portfolios, and Individual and Group Presentations
- Obtain support and involvement at the Region Level
- Promote E-Learning and ensure the involvement of highly-skilled Instructional Support Teachers with IT Skills
- Carry through a Problem-solving Process built on Trust and Collective Responsibility

LEADERSHIP REFLECTION

A Teacher expressed frustration having tried various Writing Strategies in her Classroom. Your Responsibility, as a member of the School Leadership Team, is to provide Instructional Support to the Teacher. Suggest THREE ways that the Teacher can support the Student to achieve a higher proficiency.

_____
_____
_____
_____
_____
_____
_____
_____
_____

Demonstrate TWO ways that Staff Meetings can be used to Gather Data to guide Common Instructional Planning and Adjustments, in your Educational Context

As Administrator for your School, suggest Intervention Strategies for achieving the Goals in the following Trend Analysis (Analyses) that were outlined by Colleagues in your Leadership Team:

ANALYSIS 1

The Teacher was concerned that Test Scores had fallen slightly, particularly Reading Scores for some Grades, even though the overall Grade Targets were met.

ANALYSIS 2

Failure to meet Mathematics Target for two consecutive years, based on a report presented by another Colleague, from another School.

ANALYSIS 3

An analysis of the Teacher and Office Reports that were presented by another Colleague from another School, identified Students who displayed consistent negative behaviour patterns for all Grades.

RESOURCES USED TO IMPROVE TEACHING AND LEARNING

Classroom innovations are changing the meaning of educating Students in the 21st Century. New Technologies provide understanding of how Students learn and allow Instructors to customize Course Materials and develop Personalized Learning Experiences tailored to the individual needs of Students. Today, Students are searching for Technology-driven experiences.

Kurdziolek (2011) stated that in the classroom context, Resources are referred to as Physical Demonstration Aids, Contextual Understanding of Students, Instructional Expertise, and Formal Organization of Ideas, Materials, and Activities. Instruction is a process in which knowledge collectively and collaboratively interact with these Resources and can be used as active management of Student attention that focus on Classroom Goals, such as, Classroom Management Concerns and Student Learning.

Let us reflect on what the Classroom days looked like, ages ago:
- Blackboards
- Diagrams
- Maps

School Leaders need to support Teachers in exploring the opportunities that Technology offers for improving the Quality of Classroom Instruction, including
- Access to Computer-equipped Classrooms
- Placing Notes on the Web
- Clips from the Internet, Video, Audio, News Archive
- Preparation of Multimedia Classroom Presentations
- Audio Technology integrated into Teaching

The Classroom has been changing with the advent of Modern Technology and a tech-savvy generation. Teachers in the 21st Century are enhancing the interests of Students and engaging them in Instructional Activities. Technology empowers Teachers in the Classroom, therefore, Learning should be fused with Technology. Social Media, Facebook, Twitter provide opportunities for better interaction with Students. In this information age, individuals can communicate in ways that was never imagined. Administrators and Teachers need to constantly reflect on how to incorporate Social Media in the classroom.

Let us examine the personal use of Computers in class.
Frequent checks around the classroom to determine how the Technology is being used, is important. Students take notes, view Lecture Notes on the screen during the Lesson, Email, and Surf the Internet.

It is easier for Students to grasp difficult concepts with the use of Technology. It is, therefore, important that School Leaders provide opportunities for Teachers to create individualized interventions for Diverse Learners at all levels of proficiency by enriching the Learning Environment with Technology. Leaders in Education need to ensure that Teachers become more adept in integrating Technology into the Classroom.

Let us consider assigning Students a challenging Project incorporating Multimedia. The Teacher has to ensure that they have available time to support them. It is essential that the Teacher is allowed time to learn about the Technology. While the details may not be necessary, it is important that Teachers grasp the usage of the Resources to a level that Students are comfortable using it.

Incorporating Technology in the Classroom is fundamental when ensuring an Effective Learning Environment for Students. School Leaders should encourage Teachers to utilize Technology to challenge themselves and their Students. Schools with Teachers, who are motivated and know how to use Technology Tools, will reap benefits.

DIFFERENTIATION

Many Teachers do not have the background information to commit Differentiation to Practice. Differentiation can be used to assess current levels of functioning, learning experiences, and then information used to support all Learners. It is vital for Teachers to support all Students to learn at appropriately challenging levels. Most importantly, Differentiation is the attribute for the 21st Century Teacher who is faced with multiple levels of achievement, interests, readiness, and learning styles that are present in every classroom. School Administrators can learn to differentiate Instruction more effectively with the use of Technology.

Stavroula, et al (2011) suggested that Differentiation embodies a creative, constant, and Reflective procedure of effective Teaching and Learning that is unmet with ready-made Lesson Plans. Major changes are observed in the way Teachers perceive and practice Teaching. Quality Instruction should be provided to all Students, as well as, Personal Learning leads to high levels of achievement, while at the same time, experiencing Equity. When Differentiated Instruction is implemented, the Learning Process can be enhanced, and Student Achievement improved. Differentiated Instruction is feasible, effective, and necessary for all Students. Research has proved that Differentiated Instruction has a positive effect on Student Achievement.

According to Reis, et al (2011), Educators can work with and provide materials for Students who require varied levels of difficulty, support, groupings, and different environments in the classroom by applying Differentiation of Instruction and Curriculum. The features of Successful Differentiation include:
- Curriculum or Content
- Instructional Pace
- Tangible Results

Differentiation with Enrichment is an extension of the regular Curriculum, replaced with Teacher-selected advanced content. The Teacher encourages the Student to engage in Independent Study and Topics of Personal Interest. The Teacher should, however, decide what Enrichment Types can and will be available in the classroom.

FORMAL AND INFORMAL ASSESSMENTS OF INSTRUCTIONAL EFFECTIVENESS OF TEACHERS: ALTERNATIVE APPROACHES TO SUPERVISON

"The best Mentors are the people in your life who push you just a little bit outside your comfort zone."

Leigh Cur
It is fundamental for School Leaders to learn about Alternative Approaches to Supervision and also introduce these Approaches using Reflective Practice, Interpersonal and Listening Skills, and

Collaborative Skills. Sullivan, et al (2000) argued that Inspectoral Practice is no longer valid in the 21st Century. There is an urgent need for School Administrators to demonstrate creative ways to support Classroom Teachers effectively and plan for Alternative Approaches to Supervision. In supporting the Teacher in developing all these Skills, the School Leader must provide ongoing, intensive Professional Development opportunities in an effort for these Alternative Approaches to Supervision to become a School-wide focus for improvement of Teaching and Learning.
Let us reflect on Research on Best Practices of Successful School Leadership.

The Non-judgmental Supervisory relationships that individuals form in their Education Contexts are important, sensitive, and instructional. These Non-judgmental Approaches to Supervision involve Shared Expertise and Trusted Learning. The traditional, autonomous Professionalism that are clearly outdated, has been replaced by a natural introduction of Reflective Practice and Collaboration Strategies, as exemplified by the following Approaches to Supervision:
- Coaching
- Mentoring
- Portfolios for Differentiated Supervision
- Peer Assessment

School Leaders in their personal and professional lives will encounter multiple situations where the guidance and opinion of a trusted individual can help to make the right choices. Accessing the assistance of a Mentor or a Coach can have a significant impact on how Leaders in Education perform and succeed in their lives and workplace. The terms, Coach and Mentor, are sometimes used interchangeably and assumed to be synonymous, by many.

Let us now make the distinction between Coaching and Mentoring. A Coach is an individual who helps with job-specific skills and usually more experienced with the competency and skill requirements of work. The assistance and guidance of the Coach help Teachers to carry out daily operations much smoother and enables individuals to gain the necessary experience to be able to Coach others when needed. It is often the case, where a Coach helps Teachers to survive the first few months of the job by showing ways to get the job done. A Coach, in other words, demonstrates what needs to be done, or provides advice on how to proceed. Coaching is solution-based and assists School Leaders in dealing with job-specific skills and challenges. It is not surprising that our best Coach is usually a trusted colleague performing similar duties and willing to help other individuals to progress.

Mentoring, on the other hand, helps to develop much deeper and long-term improvements by promoting Self-reflection and Skill Development. It helps us develop our career or life goals based on well thought out and intentionally utilized choices. Mentoring can help individuals become a better version of themselves through Reflection and Development. An Effective Mentor is not one who gives advice on how to respond to situations or one who articulates how a problem would be solved; rather, a Good Mentor is one who offers challenges and supports the understanding of abilities and capabilities, and one who brings out Self-initiated Actions through Self-reflection, Powerful Questions and Self-designed Action Plans. A Good Mentor also promotes accountability in commitments and choices of action. Given the complexity and long-term Goals of the Mentoring Relationship, effective Mentors are trained individuals who approach their role with the intent of seeing the Mentee grow and develop, as their main purpose. Much like the Coaching relationship, a trusting relationship must exist between the Mentor and the Mentee. Mentor relationships cannot be contrived through random assignments and pairings, as trust is a necessary prerequisite.

In Schools, Administrators, such as, Principals, Vice-principals, and Department Heads, serve the dual role of Mentor-Coach to new hires, colleagues, and staff members, and are ready and willing to develop their Job-specific, Problem-solving, and Personal Leadership Skills. School Administrators assume the roles of Coach and Mentor based on need, urgency, and time availability. Effective Mentor-Coaches teach skills and encourage Self-development and Capacity Building within their organization. Capacity Building and Leadership Development can have a profound impact on the effectiveness of a School where improving Student Learning is the ultimate Goal. Good Mentor-Coaches are not born; they are developed, value their own development, and have their own trusted Mentor-Coach who encourages them to bring out their best in their professional and personal lives. Good Mentor-Coaching develops good Mentor-Coaches.
Within an educational organization, effective and well-designed Mentor-Coaching Programmes benefit not only individuals, but the organizations served by such individuals.

Let us explore the Rationale, Potential Benefits, and Critical Components of a good Mentor-Coach Programme at an institution- or region-level.

Why would a Mentor-Coach Programme be implemented in the

Region?
- To promote the communication and realization of system intentions and values
- To allow and encourage individual growth within the context of the system vision and needs
- To develop and establish a cohesive set of standards and framework that develop individuals and strengthen the organization
- To promote Succession Planning within the organization
- To ensure that new hires are successfully inducted into the organization
- To retain and develop new hires
- To support School Improvement and increase Student Achievement

What are the attributes of an Effective Mentor-Coach Programme?
- Multiple opportunities to develop trusting relationships among Team Members
- Participants share successes and challenges
- Promotion and facilitation of Self-Reflection
- Participant-driven
- Action- and result-oriented
- Focused on learning and development
- Collaborative and supportive
- Active listening and Coaching
- Professional Networks are established and strengthened
- Instructional Leadership
- Work-life balance and Personal Wellness
- How do we achieve an effective Mentor-Coach Programme?
- Developing effective active listening techniques
- Asking powerful questions

- Coaching
- Supporting individual needs
- Aligning goals with System Improvement Plans
- Building Personal Goals and Action Plans
- Providing training on Reflective Questioning
- Addressing the needs of individual Team Members
- Providing effective and Non-judgmental Feedback
- Problem-solving specific issues as they arise
- Building safe opportunities to dialogue and to have courageous conversations
- Building trusting and self-directed relationships rather than imposed
- Coaching through Self-reflection and Conversations instead of advice
- Developing formalized checkpoints and action accountability
- Promoting confidentiality and commitment

Mentoring and Coaching Programmes, therefore, can have a great impact on how educational systems operate, and ultimately on Student Achievement, as they build and promote Teamwork, Collaboration, Alignment, Job-specific Skills and Competencies, and Trust and Relationship Building. Trained Mentor-Coaches can provide the necessary supports to deliver educational programming with intentionality and alignment with System Leaders, and Managers engaging in Collaborative Inquiries to address issues as they arise within individual settings.

Let us reflect on other Types of Supervision Assessments of the 21st Century, which may include the following:

Peer Support Groups are supported by Teachers from various Subject Areas who meet to exchange ideas relating to their Professional Goals, and also provide Support and Feedback in Self-Evaluations and general Professional Strategies and Presentations. Self-Evaluations are completed by Teachers and can range from discussing growth and development to expressing disappointments, from content-related skills to personal skills.

Peer Evaluation Teams comprise of Teachers who pool their reservoir of skills, and collaboratively produce Portfolios of any Teacher-selected Professional Work and make Presentations to School-wide Group of Peers.

Effective School Leaders create a mindset for overall School Improvement by promoting Reflection, Self-Improvement, and many others. There is need for School Administrators in the 21st Century to develop their craft as Instructional Leaders, by effectively participating in Alternative Approaches to Supervision and improving Academic Success for all Students. Implementation of more of these Alternative Approaches can lead to invaluable means to promote Professional Development; the endeavors of which will support the diverse needs of Teachers and collegiality, resulting in Schools gaining Instructional, Curricula, and Administrative benefits.

PERFORMANCE-BASED PAY

Salaries that are based on Teacher Achievements, Teacher Performance, Tasks, and Student Achievement are Performance-based Pay. If Performance-based Pay can attract the brightest into the Profession and motivate Teachers, why then does it seem like

Educators have dropped the term from their vocabulary?

How difficult is it to Evaluate Teacher Performance?

What are some potential problems with Performance-based Compensation for teachers?

How could Performance -based Compensation affect Teacher Morale?

LEADERSHIP REFLECTION

The Ministry of Education is implementing a Differential Pay System at your School. Outline THREE Challenges you would face, as Administrator, to implement this Change

_____
_____
_____
_____
_____
_____
_____
_____
_____
_____
_____
_____
_____
_____
_____
_____

How would you address a situation in your School, where Teachers successfully completed the Competency, Skills, and Knowledge Tests and are unable to demonstrate this Competency in the Classroom?

_____
_____
_____
_____
_____
_____
_____
_____
_____
_____

Comment on whether Compensation Programmes encourage Competition rather than Collaboration among Teachers.

_____
_____
_____
_____
_____
_____
_____
_____

Let us consider a recent trend to link overall School Performance to Goals instead of rewarding Teachers for Quality.

For years, the issue of Performance-based Compensation for Teachers has been a global discussion. Measuring the value of a Teacher to their Education Process is nearly impossible. What then is being measured?

Let us reflect on what constitutes a Good Teacher.
- Is the Great Teacher a Musician?
- Is the Great Teacher one with many talents?
- Is it Test Scores?
- Is it finding Scholarships for Students?
- Is it complying with Accepted School Norms?

Or should Teachers receive higher salaries for the following value-added gains:
- Attaining Advanced Degrees
- Designing Curricula
- Presenting at Workshops
- Promoting to Leadership Positions
- Mentoring and other purposeful activities

Quantitative and Qualitative Indicators are used by School Administrators to monitor performance by Teacher Observations and Reviewing Lesson Plans. Teacher Compensation should depend on Teacher Functions, in addition to Student Achievement. However, multiple measures would have to be used, such as, Portfolios and Attendance. The Subjectiveness of Performance-based Pay may not be trusted by Teachers and may need Quality Control of the Process, and if not done could create political issues.

LEADERSHIP REFLECTION

What are the Principles to be adhered to, if you were asked, as

School Administrator, to design a "Differential Pay System" for your Educational Context, as they relate to the following focus areas?

Base Pay or Variable Pay

_____
_____
_____
_____
_____
_____
_____
_____
_____
_____

Additional Benefits

_____
_____
_____
_____
_____
_____
_____
_____
_____
_____
_____

BUILDING INSTRUCTIONAL CAPACITY

Schools, Departments, and Grade-level Groups prepare the immediate environment with Instruction. School Administrators need to make available Human, Financial, and, Material Resources. Relationships develop across Classrooms and Teachers, and between School and the wider Community.

Collaborative Learning Culture is a process or practice that builds Teaching Capacity and improves Student Achievement (Ministry of Education, Ontario, Ideas into Action, Bulletin 3, 2014). School Leaders need to recognize the depth of Collaborative Learning Cultures, as it relates to Knowledge, Skills, and Persistence. Improved Working Conditions for Teachers, and Building Teacher Satisfaction and Morale are benefits of Collaborative Relaltionships, which have a positive impact on Teaching, Learning, and Student Achievement.

Let us examine the Collaborative Approaches that support Learning Communities. It is the responsibility of the School Administrators to prepare Teachers by:
- Assuring them of their beliefs to collaborate to improve Student Learning
- Remaining current through Collaborative Study
- Introducing them to participative decision-making
- Preparing others to lead
- Ensuring Data on School Performance that is available, understandable, and open to interpretation
- Encouraging them to engage in frequent dialogues and discussions

- Providing Research Opportunities on Collective Responsibilities for Student Success, Professional Refresher Courses, Peer Feedback and Assistance
- Strengthening Trust through Guided Practice in Decision-making, Conflict Management, and appropriate Dialogue.

There is a need for Schools to build a new School Culture by shifting from "Heroic" Leader to a model that focuses on Student Outcomes and increasing the number of individuals in Leadership Positions. This Shared Responsibility will have a positive impact on Students and Outcomes. The Collaborative Learning Culture focuses on the needs that best reflect on Student Achievement, which means caring for Students first when the needs of Students and Teachers conflict. Relational Trust is an essential element for School Improvement and involves transparency in relation to treatment of Staff, Students, Parents, and Community Members.

PROFESSIONAL DEVELOPMENT

Teachers should be in an environment that is cooperative, collaborative, communicative, and nurturing. Such an environment fosters trust and builds capacity. Capacity is interactive and Modelling the Skills of Collaboration is the responsibility of the School Leader. According to Ministry of Education, Ontario, Ideas into Action, Bulletin 4 (2014), Reflection is ongoing work and is an important tool for the Teacher to receive Feedback about Learning. Teachers face many challenges during the course of their day and will need to have the skills and support to deal with these situations.

Let us examine the complex work that Teachers are engaged in.

- Planning and providing an engaging Curriculum
- Communicating with Families, Colleagues, and Administration
- Responding to the ever-growing pressures of Improved Student Achievement
- Assessment
- Documentation to demonstrate Student Learning

This workload is demanding and requires the full attention of the Teacher, and School Administrators need to be cognizant of the difficulty of coping with all the expectations that are required of the Classroom Teacher. Students should be at the heart of the work of a Teacher and truly share meaningful experiences with them. Reflective Teachers need to closely observe and study the significance of the daily classroom activities, so that they can make effective purposeful decisions about how to respond to and plan for their Students. Teachers should be trained how to Reflect quickly and naturally in-the-moment in each unique situation, as they work with Students in and out of the Classroom.

School Capacity denotes knowledge, skills, and dispositions of Teachers who must be professionally competent in Instruction and Assessment. The School that employs Teachers with sound knowledge of the subject matter will select High Quality Instructional Materials. Effective School Administrators promote Professional Development as it enhances School Capacity which examines the improvement to Instruction and Student Achievement. Instructional Capacity focuses on Teachers and also crucial are Student Experiences, Understanding, Interests, Commitments, and Engagement. Leaders in Education encourage Teachers to learn more about their Students and Instructional

Materials by focusing on improved Student Performance of a particular Content.

Schools will invest in the Reflective, Thoughtful Decision-making abilities of their Teachers through Quality Programmes, such as Professional Development. School Administrators need to view Teachers as Active Collaborators by encouraging them to work in Teams frequently for extended periods of time to continue to build capacity and have access to Resources . There is a responsibility for School Leaders to provide Time, Support, Opportunities for Ongoing Reflection, Sensitivity to unique profiles of the Learner, Enjoyment, and Professional Dialogue in the change process of Raising School Standards.

A change is a difficult and slow process, and it is important that the School Administrator reinforces that small changes have the potential to make significant differences to Teaching and Student Learning. Leaders in Education need to be aware of the many clues in daily Teaching that can assist in identifying challenges in Instruction.

Let us examine some of the many Clues for Identifying Challenges in Teacher Instruction.

CHECKLIST FOR IDENTIFYING CHALLENGES IN INSTRUCTION

CLUES FOR IDENTIFYING CHALLENGES IN INSTRUCTION	YES	NO	COMMENTS
Was the Student absent for a particular Class or Activity?			
Is your lack of interest communicated to Students in this Topic?			
Does the Student understand the importance of the Content?			
Is the Lesson interactive?			
Are Students engaged at all times?			
Do Students ask questions?			
Do Students request extra Resource Materials?			
Does the Teacher check their Mood during the Lesson?			

Let us consider a Lesson demonstrating a Real-World Experience. The Teacher shared a story, asked Students to Text a Summary of the Story to a friend in the class, and then share the Summary of the Story with the Class. The Students were more attentive and now perceived the Lesson as relevant to their life and related to the Teacher since then, as a human being. It is evident that Technology has added to the many distractions that Students today, face.

Teachers need to make adjustments to their daily Reflections by analyzing their Lesson Plans and removing confusing and irrelevant information, and in addition, check for logical sequence in the Lessons taught. Keeping a Log or Journal will allow Teachers to jot down ideas, explanations, and any adjustments in the decisions of how to improve the teaching of various topics.

LEADERSHIP REFLECTION

Prepare a "Build on Successes" Checklist for Teachers in your Educational Context, who have been utilizing Techniques for Analyzing Student Learning and need to make changes to Improve their Teaching.

_____
_____
_____
_____
_____
_____
_____
_____
_____
_____
_____
_____
_____
_____
_____
_____
_____
_____
_____
_____

As a 21st Century School Administrator, how would you address the needs of your Learners that require Instructions to include the following Global Patterns:

Well-organized Lessons

_____
_____
_____
_____

Real-world Experiences

_____
_____
_____
_____

Demonstrate Respect

_____
_____
_____
_____

A good Sense of Humour

_____
_____
_____
_____

Extra Time to Respond to Questions

_____
_____

STUDENT-CENTRED OR LEARNING-CENTRED INSTRUCTION

Transitioning to Learning-Certred Instruction takes time and effort. Teachers need to build an appreciation for value of the Content taught and Teach Students how to solve real problems, which leads to the application of Content in the future. It is important that School Leaders encourage Teachers to utilize multiple Teaching Techniques appropriate for the Learning Goals and promote Student-Learning, rather than focusing on what the Teacher is doing. Students are more likely to retain Content when encouraged to explore additional content.

LEADERSHIP REFLECTION

Outline the Steps involved in supporting Teachers in your Educational Context, in developing Plan Enhancements to existing Teaching Practices

_____
_____
_____
_____
_____

Describe TWO Ways that the Responsibility of Learning is shared between Teachers and Students, in your Educational Context

_____
_____
_____
_____
_____
_____
_____
_____
_____
_____

USING TECHNOLOGY TO SUPPORT COLLABORATION

New Technologies have changed Teaching and Learning in various ways. Today, Teachers can engage their Students in Virtual Field Trips, Simulated Dissections, and Content Access in new and innovative ways. It is important that School Leaders provide opportunities for Teachers to incorporate Technology in the Classroom and create expansive use, rather than restricting the experience to obtaining information and word processing. Often times, new Technologies introduced in the Classroom are teacher-centred rather than student-centred; School Administrators in the 21st Century, need to ensure that the focus is on implementation and upgrading of new Technologies to prevent boredom.

The role of the School Leader is critical at every stage of the implementation. School Administrators can solicit support from Department Heads, Grade Supervisors, Technology Coordinators, and Special Education Team Members. Effective School Leaders recognize that for some Teachers, the thought of Technological Changes, such as, a system change to online grading system, is overwhelming and offering training and ongoing Technical support, will encourage future participation. Teachers will reach a comfort level in integrating Technology in the Classroom knowing that they have the Administration Support to succeed.

Online Technologies can provide a strong stage for Collaborative Learning. Online Communities offer opportunities for Teachers to connect with peers and share Goals, Knowledge, Capacities, and Learning Needs. According to Ministry of Education, Ontario, Ideas into Action, Bulletin 3 (2014), Web 2.0 Technologies allow for sharing of Information and Resources, utilizing various types of media. Online Communities provide social support and interactions and are channeled electronically. The Internet is a global communication Technology and is available day and night. Interactions in Online Communities are anonymous and individuals can participate effectively with Online Communication Tools, including Wikis, Discussions, Chats, and Streaming Videos. Individuals collaborate with the purpose of sharing sociability, information, and social support.

ANALYZING TEST RESULTS

When a Test is graded, the Results are used to analyze the Effectiveness of the Teacher.

Let us examine the situation where many Students responded incorrectly to a particular question, it could mean that:
- There is need for some adjustment to the teaching of that topic
- The question was not clearly worded, valid, or at the appropriate level of difficulty
- The Teacher should analyze the Test Results for the entire class and check for patterns in the responses. The School Leader needs to be skillful in ascertaining the Difficulty Level of the Test-items and also, offering Lesson Planning Supervision.

SUMMATIVE EXERCISES FOR SCHOOL ADMINISTRATORS

Develop a 5-Page Paper, describing the Vision 2030 Plan of Jamaica, as it relates to the Modules in this Text

What Gaps have you identified?

How would you address the Gaps identified, in your Educational Context?

As a Member of the School Improvement Planning Committee, how would you guide the Committee, and at the same time, remain a Working Member of the Group?

As a School Leader, Create a SWOT Analysis for your School

Create a List of Strategies that you, as School Administrator, would use to address Teacher Fears

REFERENCES

Bizmove (n.d.). The Small Business Encyclopedia: How to Conduct a Business Meeting. Retrieved from www.bizmove.com/skills/m8l.htm

Bredson, P. (2000). Support for Teacher Professional Growth and Development. Retrieved from: The School Principal's Role in Teacher Professional Development, Journal of In-Service Education, 26:2, 385-401, DOI: 10.1080/13674580000200114

California State Department of Finance (1998). Strategic Planning Guidelines. Retrieved from https://www.calhr.ca.gov/Documents/wfp-department-of-finance-strategic-plan-guidelines.pdf

Centre for Research on Learning and Teaching (2015). Guidelines for Evaluating Teaching. Retrieved from:http://www.crlt.umich.edu/tstrategies/guidelines

Changing Minds (2015). Six Emotional Leadership Styles. Retrieved from www.changingminds.org

Clarke, K. (2009). Secondary School Department Heads as Teacher Leaders: A Study in Suburban Ontario. Retrieved from https://dr.library.brocku.ca/bitstream/handle/10464/4207/Brock_Clarke_Kristen_A_2009.pdf?sequence=1

Education First (2015). Giving Teachers the Feedback and Support they Deserve: Five Essential Practices. Retrieved from www.collegeready.gatesfoundation.org

English, F. (2011). Sage Handbook of Educational Leadership: Advances in Theory, Research, and Practice (2nd ed). CA: Sage.

Farrell, K. (2011). Collegial Feedback on Teaching: A Guide to Peer Review. Retrieved from www.cshe.unimelb.edu.au

Feeney, E. (2007). Quality Feedback: The Essential Ingredient for

Student Success. Retrieved from http://www.academia.edu/6665547/Quality_Feedback_The_Essential_Ingredient_for_Teacher_Success

Fischer, C. (n.d.). Supervision of Instruction. Retrieved from http://www.stanswartz.com/adminbook/chap3.htm

Graham-Blake, J. (2002). The School Budget. Retrieved from http://paws.wcu.edu/churley/budgets.html

Growing Tomorrow's Leaders Today (n.d.). Preparing Effective School Leaders in New York State. Retireved from http://illinoisschoolleader.org/other_states/documents/ny20essential20skills20leadership.pdf

Hackmann, D. (n.d.). Distributed Leadership for Learning. Retrieved from http://documents.mx/documents/distributed-leadership-for-learning-donald-g-hackmann-university-of-illinois-at-urbana-champaign.html

Hill, R. & Matthews, P. (2008). Inspiring Leaders: Improving Children's Lives. Retrieved from http://www.curee.co.uk/files/publication/1301587364/Matthews%20evaluation%20of%20NLEs.pdf

Hurley, J. (2001). Handbook for Jamaican School Administrators. Retrieved from http://paws.wcu.edu/churley/jamaicahb.htm

Ideas into Action (2010). Promoting Collaborative Leadership Cultures: Putting the Promise into Practice, Bulletin 3. Retrieved from https://www.edu.gov.on.ca/eng/policyfunding/memos/july2010/Bulletin3_Spring2010.pdf

Ideas into Action (2014). Setting Goals: The Power of Purpose, Bulletin 4. Retrieved from https://www.edu.gov.on.ca/eng/policyfunding/leadership/IdeasIntoActionBulletin4.pdf

Ideas into Action (2014). Aligning Resources with Priorities:

Focusing on What Matters Most, Bulletin 6. Retrieved from http://www.edu.gov.on.ca/eng/policyfunding/leadership/IdeasInto ActionBulletin6.pdf

Kurdziolek, M. (2011). Classroom Resources and Impact on Learning. Retrieved from http://www.lookebooks.org/pdf/classroom-resources-and-impact-on-learning.html

Leithwood, K., Louis, K., Anderson, S., & Wahlstrom, K. (2014). How Leadership Influences Student Learning. Retrieved from http://www.wallacefoundation.org/knowledge-center/school-leadership/key-research/Pages/How-Leadership-Influences-Student-Learning.aspx

Leithwood, K., Day, C., Sammons, P., Harris, A., & Hopkins, D. (2006). Successful School Leadership: What it is and how it Influences Pupil Learning. Retrieved from http://illinoisschoolleader.org/research_compendium/documents/successful_school_leadership.pdf

Leithwood, K., Louis, K., Anderson, S., & Wahlstrom, K. (2004). How Leadership Influences Student Learning. http://www.wallacefoundation.org/knowledge-center/school-leadership/key-research/Pages/How-Leadership-Influences-Student-Learning.aspx

Lewis, D., Madison-Harris, R., Muoneke, A., & Times, C. (2009). Using Data to Guide Instruction and Improve Student Learning. Retrieved from www.sedl.org/pubs/sedl-letter/v22n02/using-data.html

Martin, S. (2009). Relationship between the Leadership Styles of Principals and School Culture. Retrieved from http://digitalcommons.georgiasouthern.edu/cgi/viewcontent.cgi?article=1269&context=etd

Mulford, B. (2003). School Leaders: Challenging Roles and Impact on Teacher and School Effectiveness. Retrieved from http://www.oecd.org/edu/school/37133393.pdf

Paranosic, N. (2014). The "Fifth Business" of Department Heads: Examining the Perceptions of Department Heads about their Role. Electronic Thesis and Dissertation Repository. Paper 2468.

Pont, B., Nusche, D., & Moorman, H. (2008). Improving School Leadership: Volume1: Policy and Practice. Retrieved from https://books.google.com.jm/books?hl=en&lr=&id=1OvVAgAAQBAJ&oi=fnd&pg=PA17&dq=Improving+School+Leadership:+Volume1:+Policy+and+Practice.&ots=buzqnw2jC_&sig=a1nWcf_nxWNl_F2K5cB93IBOZjM&redir_esc=y#v=onepage&q=Improving%20School%20Leadership%3A%20Volume1%3A%20Policy%20and%20Practice.&f=false

Prescott, D. (2011). Resolving Classroom Management and School Leadership Issues in ELT. Retrieved from http://www.cambridgescholars.com/download/sample/60247

Reis, S. & Renzulli, J. (2011). Compass Learning: White Paper on Differentiation. Retrieved from http://confratute.uconn.edu/wp-content/uploads/sites/990/2015/07/Compass-Five_Dimensions-Renzulli.pdf

Ryan, C. (2014). Outcomes of Incorporating E-Learning in School VET Delivery: How has Gen Y benefitted from the 1:1 Laptop Programme. Retrieved from http://avetra.org.au/wp-content/uploads/2014/05/Abstract-111.pdf

Seifert, E. & Vornberg, J. (2002). The New School Leader for the 21st Century: Principal: Retrieved from https://books.google.com.jm/books?id=-2Oy1Kcvm8sC&pg=PP1&lpg=PP1&dq=The+New+School+Leader+for+the+21st+Century:+Principal&source=bl&ots=yKA9cxQIZZ&sig=6ytx-bz4akoXiD79ANaj_HMY1GE&hl=en&sa=X&ved=0ahUKEwik9-

jkvMPJAhVB7D4KHalSChUQ6AEINTAF#v=onepage&q=The%20New%20School%20Leader%20for%20the%2021st%20Century%3A%20Principal&f=false

Sohan, D. (2002). How Principals Develop and Administer a School Budget. Retrieved from http://paws.wcu.edu/churley/budgets.html

Stavroula, V., Leonidas, K., & Koutselini, M. (2011). Investigating the Impact of Differentiated Instruction in Mixed Ability Classrooms: Its Impact on the Quality and Equity Dimensions of Educational Effectiveness. http://www.icsei.net/icsei2011/Full%20Papers/0155.pdf

Sullivan, S. & Glanz, J. (2000). "Alternative Approaches to Supervision: Cases from the Field," The Journal of Curriculum and Supervision 15: 212-235.

The Cross Sectoral Assessment Working Party (2011). Teachers' Guide to Assessment. Retrieved from http://www.det.act.gov.au/__data/assets/pdf_file/0011/297182/Teachers_Guide_to_Assessment_Web.pdf

The Leadership Framework for Principals and Vice Principals (2014). Retrieved from https://www.edu.gov.on.ca/eng/policyfunding/leadership/PVPLeadershipFramework.pdf

The Ontario Leadership Framework (2013). A School and System Leader's Guide to Putting Ontario Leadership Framework into Action. Retrieved from https://iel.immix.ca/storage/6/1380680840/OLF_User_Guide_FINAL.pdf

Weller, L. & Weller, S. (2001). The Assistant Principal. Leadership Knowledge and Skills: The Essentials for Effectiveness. Retrieved from http://www.corwin.com/upm-data/7330_weller_ch_1.pdf

West Virginia Department of Education (n.d.). Strategic Leadership: Summary. Retrieved from http://wvde.state.wv.us/principalsinstitute/institute07-08/docs/leadership_practices_inventory.pdf

White, J. (n.d.). Characteristics of Successful Pastors. Retrieved from http://www.tntemple.edu/application/files/Academics/DMin/J.White.pdf

Whitney, D. et al (n.d.). Focus on What Works to Drive Winning Performance and Build a Thriving Organization. Retrieved from http://positivechange.org/five-strategies-of-appreciative-leadership/

CONTRIBUTORS' PAGE

Paul Panayi is a practising Ontario Educator for the last 30 years. His experiences include teaching Mathematics and Science and being a Secondary School Administrator for the last 14 years. His interests focus on Leadership Development at the School and District levels, Instructional Leadership, Growth Mindset and its application to Assessment Practices in Schools, and the development of Mentor-Coaching Programmes for School Leaders. He has been involved with the design and delivery of multiple Programmes at the School and District levels and works with and through others to improve Student Learning and Achievement. In addition, he is an active member of the Thames Valley Ontario Principals' Council Executive over the last 5 years, serving in various capacities and as its President during the 2013-2014 School Year.

Chris Friesen has been a Secondary School Administrator within the Thames Valley DSB for 15 years. He also has been an administrator within Adult and Continuing Education. He has experience and expertise in Enrichment/Gifted Programming, Strategic Planning, Student Leadership and Voice, Parent and Student Engagement, and Special Needs. Beyond this experience, Chris has led initiatives in Child Welfare at the Local and Provincial Levels, as well as, serving on the local Children's Aid Board of Directors for 14 years, three of those as Chair of the

Board.

Very active in his community, he is the Chair of the Children's Aid Foundation, Chair of the Crown Ward Education Championship Team, and Chair of the Future Oxford Partnership which will be implementing the Community Sustainability Plan.

OTHER BOOKS BY HEATHER THANE

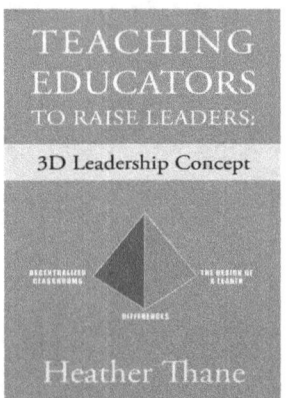

"Unlock your Greatness Leadership Coaches' Manual"

This accompanying manual is an invaluable resource tool. It appeals not just to the intellect, but to the heart and the emotions plus the will upon which everything depends. It contains helpful activities for reflective thinking and for guiding the thought in the decision making process. The lessons contained herein are so designed to involve and engage students to facilitate discovery learning. The strategic questions asked and the suggested activities capitalize on the different levels of higher order learning. Students cannot help but get the right impression that using their potential and abilities innovatively; they can make a positive contribution to the solution of the world's problems.

"I am a Leader Coaches'Manual"

This manual is punctuated with very practical and helpful strategies in the implementation of its counterpart handbook text. Its holistic approach leads the mind of the student along a path that is designed to bring about a transforming experience. It has the potential of making a great inspirational impact on teachers. It is aimed at developing the skills and boosting the motivation, as well as, clarifying the approach teachers and coaches need to be successful in their roles as change agents in the field of education. Clear attainable goals and practical step-by-step directions are delineated in almost every page. This text clarifies the role of leadership in a manner easily understood with clear, simple, relevant examples and illustrations. It will most certainly give purposeful, enjoyable and meaningful implementation to the teacher.

Saul Leacock BSc (SW), M.Ed (Psy).

President, Barbados Association of Guidance Counsellors

ABOUT THE AUTHOR

Heather Thane is an author, editor, educational consultant, and former teacher at all levels of the education sector in both Canada and the Caribbean. She is currently the President and Founder of Leadership and Beyond Educational Consultancy, dedicated to training School Administrators and Teachers, globally. Heather holds a Master's Degree in Education from Nova Southeastern University, Florida.

Heather's expertise in Educational Leadership has led to her publishing five books, endorsed by UNICEF, which has provided her with many professional development opportunities to train School Leaders and Teachers in Jamaica and the Caribbean. Her titles include: Unlock your Greatness Leadership Coaches' Manual, I am a Leader Coaches' Manual, Teaching Educators to Raise Leaders: 3D Leadership Concept, Raising Leaders in the Classroom: A Student-Teacher Handbook, Leadership Strategies for Secondary School Teachers, and Dynamics of Educational Leadership: Team Building Skills for the School Administrator, the latter to be published in the next quarter. She resides in Canada, where the snow scenery inspires her writing.

www.ingramcontent.com/pod-product-compliance
Lightning Source LLC
Chambersburg PA
CBHW061446300426
44114CB00014B/1855